Me and **White** Supremacy

How to Recognise Your
Privilege, Combat Racism
and Change the World

LAYLA F SAAD

QUERCUS

Hardback edition published in Great Britain in 2020 by Quercus Editions Ltd

This paperback edition published in 2022 by

QUERCUS

Quercus Editions Ltd
Carmelite House
50 Victoria Embankment
London EC4Y 0DZ

An Hachette UK company

A CIP catalogue record for this book is available
from the British Library

PB ISBN 978 1 52940 511 8
Ebook ISBN 978 1 52940 508 8

Every effort has been made to contact copyright holders. However, the publishers will be glad to
rectify in future editions any inadvertent omissions brought to their attention.

Quercus Editions Ltd hereby exclude all liability to the extent permitted by law for any errors
or omissions in this book and for any loss, damage or expense (whether direct or indirect)
suffered by a third party relying on any information contained in this book.

First published in the United States in 2020 by Sourcebooks.

The author appreciates The Circle Way's spirit of generosity allowing people access
to their information and practice. Its inclusion in this book does not indicate endorsement.
Readers are encouraged to explore thecircleway.net to find other open materials and to read the book,
The Circle Way: A Leader in Every Choir (Barrett-Koehler Publishers, San Francisco, 2010).

Originally published as *The Me and White Supremacy Workbook* in 2019 by Layla Saad.

10 9 8 7 6 5 4

Printed and bound in Great Britain by Clays Ltd, Elcograf S.p.A.

MIX
Paper from
responsible sources
FSC® C104740

Papers used by Quercus are from well-managed forests and other responsible sources.

For Sam, Maya, and Mohamed.
Thank you for loving me, believing in me,
and inspiring me to be a good ancestor.

I love you.
This is for you.

To shape God
With wisdom and forethought
To benefit your world,
Your people,
Your life,
Consider consequences
Minimize harm
Ask questions,
Seek answers,
Learn,
Teach.

Earthseed: The Books of the Living I,
Verse 43; Octavia Butler, *Parable of the Talents*

contents

foreword

BY ROBIN DIANGELO

"All right!" you say. "I get it! Now what do I do?"

I am a white antiracist educator. Invariably, the number one question I am asked by a white participant at the end of a presentation is "What do I do?" It may seem a reasonable thing to ask upon realizing that you are complicit in white supremacy. Yet this question is problematic. First and foremost, it is problematic because I believe it is disingenuous. It has been my consistent experience leading antiracist education over the last twenty-five years that most white people don't really *want* to know what to do about racism if it will require anything of them that is inconvenient or uncomfortable.

Indeed, asking this question is often a way to mitigate or deflect feelings of racial discomfort. While the racist status quo is comfortable for me virtually twenty-four-seven as a white person, challenging the racist status quo is not. Building the racial stamina required to challenge the racist status quo is thus a critical part of our work as white people. Rushing ahead to solutions—especially when we have barely begun to think critically about the problem—bypasses the necessary personal work and reflection and distances us from understanding our own complicity. In fact, racial discomfort is *inherent* to an authentic examination of white supremacy. By avoiding this discomfort, the racist status quo is protected.

The entitled demand for simple answers also allows us to dismiss the information if those answers are not forthcoming ("She didn't tell us what to do!"). This is especially arrogant when the demand is made of Black, Indigenous, and People of Color (BIPOC). In essence we are saying, "You do all the work and take all the risk, then hand me the fruits of your labor. I will sit back and receive them while taking no personal risk myself." And what happens when we don't like those answers because they are not quick, convenient, or comfortable? When the answers challenge our self-image as open-minded progressive individuals, free of all racial conditioning? As BIPOC have experienced again and again, when we don't agree with the answers we have demanded, we all too often feel qualified to dismiss them.

White supremacy is arguably the most complex social system of the last several hundred years. If only the answer was to be nice and keep smiling! But, of course, there are no easy answers for ending white supremacy.

In my effort to answer to the question of what to do next, I have begun to ask a counter question: "How have you managed not to know?" In the era of Google and social media, the information on what white people can do about racism is everywhere, and BIPOC have been telling us what they need for a very long time. Why haven't we sought out the information on our own up until now? Why haven't we looked it up, as we would have done for any other topic that interested us? Asking white people why they don't already know the answer is meant to be a challenge to the apathy about white supremacy that I have come to believe most white people feel. But it is also a sincere question. If we actually made a list of why we don't know what to do, we would have a guide for moving forward. Nothing on that guide would be simple or easy to change, but change would be possible. Your list might look something like this:

- I wasn't educated about racism.

- I don't talk about racism with other white people.

- I don't talk about racism with the People of Color in my life.

- I don't have People of Color in my life.

- I don't want to feel guilty.

- I haven't cared enough to find out.

Layla F. Saad has given us a road map for addressing each of the above points, as well as for addressing all of the dynamics I have raised, and more. This book is a gift of compassion from a brilliant Black woman willing to guide you through a deep examination of white racial conditioning in service of your liberation. *Me and White Supremacy* is an extraordinary new resource for white people willing to align what they profess to value (racial equality) with their actual practice (antiracist action). In a clear and accessible way, Saad has answered the question. Now, each time I am asked by a white person, "What do I do?", my answer will include "Work through this book."

PART I

welcome to the work

Dear Reader,

How did you feel the first time you saw the title of this book? Were you surprised? Confused? Intrigued? Uncomfortable? Maybe all of the above? I want to begin by reassuring you that all those feelings and more are completely normal. This is a simple and straightforward book, but it is not an easy one. Welcome to the work.

I'm Layla, and for (at least!) the next twenty-eight days, I'm going to be guiding you on a journey to help you explore and unpack your relationship with white supremacy. This book is a one-of-a-kind personal antiracism tool structured to help people with white privilege understand and take ownership of their participation in the oppressive system of white supremacy. It is designed to help them take responsibility for dismantling the way that this system manifests, both within themselves and within their communities.

The primary force that drives my work is a passionate desire to become a good ancestor. My purpose is to help create change, facilitate healing, and seed new possibilities for those who will come after I am gone. This book is a contribution to that purpose. It is a resource that I hope will help you do the internal and external work needed to become a good ancestor too. To leave this world in a better place than you have found it. The system of white supremacy was not created by anyone who is alive today. But it is maintained and upheld by everyone who holds white privilege—whether or not you want it or agree with it. It is my desire that this book will help you to question, challenge, and dismantle this system that has hurt and killed so many Black, Indigenous, and People of Color (BIPOC).

This book began as a free twenty-eight-day Instagram challenge, which then became a free digital PDF workbook downloaded by more than one hundred thousand people around the world. And now it sits in your hands as a published book, which I hope will serve as a trusty companion that you will carry in your metaphorical antiracism backpack.

This book is part education, part activation. You will find yourself expanding your intellectual and emotional understanding of racism and white supremacy, but more importantly, you will find yourself doing the work as an individual to help dismantle it. This book will help you take a clear look at different multifaceted aspects of white supremacy and how they operate in both subtle and direct ways within you and within others. It acts as a mirror being held up to you so that you can deeply examine how you have been complicit in a system that has been purposely designed to benefit you through unearned privileges at the expense of BIPOC. This book is for people who are ready to do the work, people who want to create change in the world by activating change within themselves first.

We are at a very important time in history. Many white liberal progressives like to believe that we are in a postracial time in history. But the truth is, racism and anti-Blackness are still alive and well today. BIPOC are suffering daily from the effects of historic and modern colonialism. Right-wing, anti-Muslim nationalism is gaining popularity across the Western world. And anti-Blackness continues to be a form of racism that can be found all around the world. It may seem like we are at a time in history when racism and white supremacy are resurfacing, but the truth is, they never went away. So while it is true that events in recent history, such as the 2016 U.S. presidential election, have brought these issues to the forefront, the reality is that these issues have always been there. And BIPOC in white-dominated societies and spaces have been at the receiving end of constant discrimination, inequities, injustices, and aggressions.

More people with white privilege are learning about racial dynamics and social justice terminologies than ever before. They are awakening to the fact that their white privilege has protected them from having to understand what it means to navigate the world as a BIPOC and to the ways in which they have unintentionally caused harm to BIPOC through racial aggressions. This book is here to change that. It is here to wake you up by getting you to tell the truth. This work is not about those white people "out there."

It is about you. Just you.

It is important to understand that this is deep, raw, challenging, personal, heartbreaking, *and* heart-expanding work. This book will challenge you in ways that you have not been challenged before. But we are living in challenging times. There is much work to be done. And it begins with getting honest with yourself, getting educated, becoming more conscious about what is really going on (and how you are complicit in it), and getting uncomfortable as you question your core paradigms about race. If you are willing to do that, and if we are all committed to doing the work that is ours to do, we have a chance of creating a world and way of living that are closer to what we all desire for ourselves and one another.

This work sounds overwhelming, intimidating, and unrewarding. I won't lie to you: it is. You will become overwhelmed when you begin to discover the depths of your internalized white supremacy. You will become intimidated when you begin to realize how this work will necessitate seismic change in your life. You will feel unrewarded because there will be nobody rushing to thank you for doing this work. But if you are a person who believes in love, justice, integrity, and equity for all people, then you know that this work is nonnegotiable. If you are a person who wants to become a good ancestor, then you know that this work is some of the most important work that you will be called to do in your lifetime.

Here's to doing what is right and not what is easy.

a little about me

As we are going to be spending quite an extended time together doing very deep and vulnerable work, I think it is important for you to know a little about me—your guide—before we begin.

The first thing to know about me is that I sit at a number of different intersections of identities and experiences at the same time. I am a Black woman. More specifically, I am an East African and Middle Eastern Black woman. I am a Muslim woman. I am a British citizen. I live in Qatar. And I speak, write, and teach to a global audience.

My parents immigrated to the United Kingdom from Zanzibar and Kenya in the 1970s, and that is where they met and married. My two younger brothers and I were born and spent the early years of our childhood in Cardiff, Wales, later moving to Swindon, England, and then onward to Doha, Qatar, where I still live today. My father, who is now coming close to retirement, spent his entire career sailing around the world as a mariner. He would travel to far-off places and bring us back gifts and stories from other countries. Importantly, he instilled in my brothers and me a philosophy of being citizens of the world. This idea that there is nowhere in the world where we do not belong and that we do not have to be confined to anyone's attempts to label or define us has been one that has stayed with me to this day. My incredible mother took on the Herculean task of being two parents to my siblings and me during the long months when my father was working at sea. She was dedicated to creating an environment in our home where our cultural identities and our religious beliefs were nurtured and practiced. The loving foundation she laid in those years of our childhood still stands strong today.

And yet, every time we left the house, every time we went to school, every time we watched TV, every time we connected with the rest of the world, we were interacting with white supremacy. Every day, in little and not-so-little ways, we were reminded that we were "other." That we were less than those who held white privilege. I can count on one hand the number of times I experienced overt racism. But in countless subtle ways, every day, it was felt indirectly. And those indirect messages—from being treated slightly differently by schoolteachers, to hardly ever seeing fictional characters or media representations that looked like me, to understanding that I would have to work a lot harder than my white peers to be treated the same, to understanding that my needs were always an afterthought (why could I never find a foundation shade that matched me exactly while my white friends always could?)—painted an indelible picture in my mind. A picture that taught me this: Black girls like me did not matter in a white world. I will spend the rest of my life tearing down this picture and painting a new one that reflects the truth: Black girls matter. Everywhere.

Across my lifetime, I have lived in three different continents: Europe, Africa, and Asia. I have spent just over half of that time living outside the Western world, but that does not mean that the effects of white supremacy have not continued to impact me. I want to be very clear that though I am a Black Muslim woman, I also have a lot of privilege. I do not live in a white supremacist society. The religion I practice is the national religion of the country I live in. I have socioeconomic, cisgender, heterosexual, able-bodied, neurotypical, and educational privileges. I have not experienced and cannot speak to the depth of pain that Black people who are descendants of enslaved people across the diaspora experience through racism. Living in the Middle East, I am not exposed to the more direct experience of institutional racism that my younger brothers and my niece and nephew are exposed to living in the United Kingdom. However, the childhood that I had growing up as a Black Muslim girl in a primarily white, Christian society influenced my self-development and self-concept in negative ways. And as an adult, on the worldwide internet, where more than 50 percent of the world's population spends their time and where I do my work, I am exposed to white supremacy every day.

As someone who shares her work with a global audience (the majority of my readers and podcast listeners are in North America, the U.K., across Europe, Australia, and New Zealand), I face the inevitable white fragility that comes with being a Black Muslim woman with a voice. Not living in a Western country does not protect me from getting abusive emails or social media messages for doing the work that I do.

But still, you may be asking, "Why you?"

As someone who does not live in a white-dominated society and who does not carry a lineage of the horrors of the enslavement of my ancestors, why have I chosen to do the work of writing this book and facilitating this work? Why does dismantling white supremacy matter so much to me?

It matters to me because I am a Black woman. My work is born out of both the pain and the pride of being a Black woman. It is painful to me to know how BIPOC like me are seen and treated because of our skin color. At the same time, I feel incredibly proud to stand in the fullness of who I am as a Black woman and to support other BIPOC to do the same for themselves, too, by dismantling the system that has prevented us from doing so.

I do this work because white supremacy has negatively impacted how I see myself and how the world sees and treats me. I do this work because white supremacy will negatively impact my children and my descendants: how they see themselves and how the world will see and treat them. I do this work because I belong to the global family of the African diaspora, and it hurts me that Black people around the world are treated as inferior because of our skin color. I do this work because People of Color everywhere deserve to be treated with dignity and respect, something that white supremacy strips them of. I do this work because I have a voice, and it is my responsibility to use my voice to dismantle a system that has hurt me and that hurts BIPOC every day. I do this work because I was called to it, and I answered that call.

The concepts that I have brought together in this book begin from my own personal lived experiences (both as a child and as an adult, regardless of where I have physically lived in the world). And they are deepened and further illustrated by drawing on examples from experiences I have witnessed, historical contexts, cultural moments, fictional and nonfictional literature, the media, and more. I am just one Black Muslim woman contributing to the mountains of work and labor that have already been contributed to dismantle white supremacy by BIPOC who are far more courageous and have risked far more than I have, all over the world for centuries. It is a humbling honor to have the privilege to add to this global and collective body of work.

It is my hope that this work—which is a combination of learning and reflective journaling—will create a deep shift in consciousness and action within you to help create a world without white supremacy.

what is white supremacy?

White supremacy is a racist ideology that is based upon the belief that white people are superior in many ways to people of other races and that therefore, white people should be dominant over other races.[1] White supremacy is not just an attitude or a way of thinking. It also extends to how systems and institutions are structured to uphold this white dominance. For the purposes of this book, we are only going to be exploring and unpacking what white supremacy looks like at the personal and individual level. However, since systems and institutions are created and held in place by many individual people, it is my hope that as more people do the personal inner work in here, there will be a ripple effect of actionable change of how white supremacy is upheld out there. This work is therefore not just about changing how things look but how things actually are—from the inside out, one person, one family, one business, and one community at a time.

Perhaps you are wondering why I chose to use the words *white supremacy* for this book and not something softer or less confrontational like *Me and White Privilege* or *Me and Unconscious Bias*. It would certainly have made picking up this book at the bookstore or sharing it with your family and friends less awkward! People often think that white supremacy is a term that is only used to describe far-right extremists and neo-Nazis. However, this idea that white supremacy only applies to the so-called "bad ones" is both incorrect and dangerous, because it reinforces the idea that white supremacy is an ideology that is only upheld by a fringe group of white people. White supremacy is far from fringe. In white-centered societies and communities, it is the dominant paradigm that forms the foundation from which norms, rules, and laws are created.

Many white people hear the words *white supremacy* and think *That doesn't apply to me,* that they don't hold that belief but rather that they believe that all of us are equal and that they don't modify their treatment of people based on the color of their skin. What this book, which is a deep-diving self-reflection tool, will help you to realize, however, is that that isn't true. White supremacy is an ideology, a paradigm, an institutional system, and a worldview that you have been born into by virtue of your white privilege. I am not talking about the physical color of your skin being inherently bad or something to feel shame about. I am talking about the historic and modern legislating, societal conditioning, and systemic institutionalizing of the construction of whiteness as inherently superior to people of other races. Yes, outwardly racist systems of oppression like chattel slavery, apartheid, and racial discrimination in employment have been made illegal. But the subtle and overt discrimination, marginalization, abuse, and killing of BIPOC in white-dominated communities continues even today because white supremacy continues to be the dominant paradigm under which white societies operate.

So we must call a thing a thing.

We must look directly at the ways in which this racist ideology of white supremacy, this idea that white equals better, superior, more worthy, more credible, more deserving, and more valuable actively harms anyone who does not own white privilege.

If you are willing to dare to look white supremacy right in the eye and see yourself reflected back, you are going to become better equipped to dismantle it within yourself and within your communities.

White supremacy is a system you have been born into. Whether or not you have known it, it is a system that has granted you unearned privileges, protection, and power. It is also a system that has been designed to keep you asleep and unaware of what having that privilege, protection, and power has meant for people who do not look like you. What you receive for your whiteness comes at a steep cost for those who are not white. This may sicken you and cause you to feel guilt, anger, and frustration. But you cannot change your white skin color to stop receiving these privileges, just like BIPOC cannot change their skin color to stop receiving racism. But what you *can* do is wake up to what is really going on. I invite you to challenge your complicity in this system and work to dismantle it within yourself and the world.

who is this work for?

This work is for any person who holds white privilege. By *any person*, I mean persons of any gender identity, including gender-nonconforming persons, and by *who holds white privilege*, I mean persons who are visually identifiable as white or who pass for white. Therefore, this includes persons who are biracial, multiracial, or white-passing People of Color who benefit under systems of white supremacy from having lighter skin color than visibly Brown, Black, or Indigenous people.

Important note for biracial, multiracial, and People of Color who hold white privilege: This work is for you too. However, your experience of doing this work will be very different from the experiences of white people who are not biracial, multiracial, or People of Color. While you receive the benefits of white privilege from being lighter skinned or white passing, that does not mean you have had the same experiences as a white person. You might have white parent(s) or other ancestors. Or perhaps you are not white at all but are instead a Person of Color who is lighter skinned, white passing, or white adjacent. Your white privilege does not erase or minimize your other identities or experiences. So while it is important for you to do the work to address your internalized white supremacy and white privilege, you will need to adjust the questions to better fit your experiences as a person who holds white privilege but is not white. Depending on your specific white privilege, some journal prompts will take you deeper than others. Some journal prompts will be more directly applicable to you than others.

It is also important to know that this work will bring up some challenging feelings around your internalized oppression against yourself and your marginalized identities and about how you have also been oppressed by a system that only benefits you to the extent that you are able to present or pass as white and be anti-Black.

This work will likely bring up many conflicting emotions including shame, confusion, fear, anger, remorse, grief, and anxiety. This work will bring up dynamics that have caused you or others harm in your family relationships, friendships, romantic relationships, or work relationships. Please prioritize your self-care as you move through this work. Do not use it as an excuse to not do the work in a substantial way, but at the same time, honor yourself and the different feelings that show up around your identities. Do not use this work as a stick to beat yourself with, but rather use it to interrogate your complicity within a system of privilege that is only designed to benefit you to the extent that you can conform to the rules of whiteness.

what you will need
to do this work

You will need three things for this work:

your truth
your love
your commitment

YOUR TRUTH

This is truth work. Tell the truth, as deeply as you can. No side-stepping or surface skimming. The more you tell the truth, the deeper this work takes you. What you will get out of this work is what you put into it. If you stay at the surface, what you receive from this work (and consequently what you will put out into the world as antiracist practice) will be surface level. If you go deep, if you tell the real, raw, ugly truths so you can get to the rotten core of your internalized white supremacy, what you get out of this work and put out into the world will be beyond transformational.

I cannot emphasize this enough: This work is not an intellectual exercise or a mental thought experiment. When we talk about racism, we are talking about people's lives. This is not a personal growth book that is designed to make you feel good about yourself. It is likely that in doing this work consistently, you will find some level of personal healing. However, I want to make it very clear that this is not the purpose of this work. The purpose is the healing and restored dignity of BIPOC. This work is designed to help you to be and do better by BIPOC in your communities, and that requires you to tell the truth with integrity and depth. When you don't tell the truth as deeply as you can, you are cheating yourself of your own growth, cheating BIPOC of your allyship, and illustrating that you are not truly committed to dismantling white supremacy within yourself and therefore within the world.

YOUR LOVE

This is love work. Love is one of those words that is hard to define. But in the context of this work, here is what it means to me: It means that you do this work because you believe in something greater than your own self-gain. It means you do this work because you believe that every human being deserves dignity, freedom, and equality. It means you do this work because you desire wholeness for yourself and for the world. It means you do this work because you want to become a good ancestor. It means you do this work because love is not a verb to you but an action. It means you do this work because you no longer want to intentionally or unintentionally harm BIPOC.

You will also need love for this journey because when the truth telling gets really hard, you will need something more powerful than pain and shame to encourage you to keep going. Pain and shame are neither desirable nor sustainable as long-term strategies for transformational change. It is my hope that love is what initially brought you to this work. It is my conviction that love is what will keep you going.

YOUR COMMITMENT

This is commitment work. This work is hard. There is no way to sugarcoat it. White supremacy is an evil. It is a system of oppression that has been designed to give you benefits at the expense of the lives of BIPOC, and it is living inside you as unconscious thoughts and beliefs. The process of examining it and dismantling it will necessarily be painful. It will feel like waking up to a virus that has been living inside you all these years that you never knew was there. And when you begin to interrogate it, it will fight back to protect itself and maintain its position.

There is nothing I can do to protect you from that. There are no safety nets, no shortcuts, and no easier routes. You will want to close the book, run away, and pretend you never heard of me. You will want to blame me, rage at me, discredit me, and list all the reasons why you are a good person and why you don't need to do this work.

That is a normal, expected response. That is the response of the white fragility and anti-Blackness lying inside. You have to understand this before you begin. You have to understand that this is what you can expect to occur. And you have to decide now before you begin, and then again throughout the work, that you are going to stay committed regardless. You have to decide what is going to be the anchor that keeps you committed to this work, whether it is a commitment to antioppression and the dignity of BIPOC, your commitment to your own healing, your commitment to being a better friend or family member to BIPOC, or your commitment to your own personal or spiritual values. Decide now, before you begin, what is going to help you stay committed to this work when the going gets tough.

What keeps me going is my commitment to truth, love, and being a good ancestor.

how to use
this book

Here are some tips for using this book as a self-guided journey.

Keep a Journal

This is a book that is designed for you not just to read but to work
through. The best way to do that is to purchase a journal to use for
working through each day's journal prompts. You will want to refer
back to your journal reflections and notes again and again as you do
the lifelong work of antiracism.

Go at Your Own Pace

While it has been designed as a twenty-eight-day challenge, you
absolutely do not have to complete this work within twenty-eight
days. You can go through this book at your own pace, as fast or as
slow as you choose. Remember: it's not a race, it's a journey.

Don't Generalize

When answering the prompts, do not generalize about white people broadly. Do not talk about white people as if you are not a white person or as if you do not benefit from white privilege. Remember this book is about your own personal experiences, thoughts, and beliefs, not those of other people.

For Your First Time, Work Sequentially

If this is your first time working through this book, I suggest working through it sequentially, as each prompt builds upon the preceding one.

After Your First Time, Work Intuitively

After completing all twenty-eight days, you can go back and use it intuitively or in a way that works best for you. You can either begin again from Day 1, or you can dip in and out depending on what particular aspect of white supremacy is coming up for you to explore at that time.

Work Alone or with a Group

You can use this book alone or work through it with a group of people who are also doing this work. See the Resources section at the end of this book for more specific guidance on how to do this work in a group setting in a *Me and White Supremacy* book circle (page 211).

Keep Asking Questions

As you move through the book answering each prompt to the best of your ability, dig deeper by asking yourself when, how, and why questions. For example: *When do I react this way? When do these thoughts or feelings come up for me? How does this specific aspect of white supremacy show up for me? How does thinking or feeling this way benefit me? Why do I feel this way? Why do I believe this? Why do I think this is true? Why do I hold on to these beliefs?* Asking when, how, and why will help you to get down into the deeper unconscious layers of your internalized white supremacy, thus taking your work a lot deeper.

self-care, support, and sustainability

As this work is challenging, it is important to say a little bit about self-care, support, and sustainability.

Many people who did the live twenty-eight-day Instagram challenge found this work physically, emotionally, and spiritually challenging. As you root out your internalized white supremacy, your body, mind, and spirit will be affected. To ensure that you are able to sustain the work, make sure to prioritize your self-care. I'm not talking about manicures and trips to the spa. I'm talking about doing what you need to stay grounded in yourself, connected to your body, and emotionally well.

If you are the only person in your family, friend group, or community doing this work, it can feel lonely. Reach out to other people who are doing this work so that you can support one another. Be mindful, however, of not leaning on BIPOC (whether family, friends, or peers) to support you and help you process what is coming for you unless they consciously consent to holding that space for you. This kind of support is a form of emotional labor that is very taxing for BIPOC.

Challenging emotions like shame, anger, grief, rage, apathy, anxiety, and confusion will come up for you if you are doing this work deeply. Don't run away from those feelings. Feeling the feelings—which are an appropriate human response to racism and oppression—is an important part of the process. When you allow yourself to feel those feelings, you wake up. You rehumanize yourself. You start to realize that you weren't feeling these feelings before because you had shut down a part of your humanity in order to participate in white supremacy. White supremacy purposely numbs you to the pain that your racism causes. Doing this work brings back the real feelings of pain of what committing racism actually feels like physically, mentally, emotionally, and spiritually.

The purpose of this work is not for you to end up living in shame. The purpose is to get you to see the truth so that you can do something about it. No matter how bad it feels to wake up to the pain, shame, and guilt of your racism, those feelings will never come anywhere close to the pain BIPOC experience as a result of your racism. So instead of getting stuck or overwhelmed, channel those feelings into action and change. Talking to a friend, family member, support group, therapist, or coach will be helpful in supporting you to process what is coming up for you so you can keep moving forward.

Audre Lorde said, "Revolution is not a one-time event." Antiracism work is not a twenty-eight-day journey. It is a lifelong practice. This book presents a place to begin and to continue the work. But it requires your lifelong commitment to antioppression. This is not like reading a personal growth book, attending a spiritual retreat, or going to a wellness conference. There is no feel-good reward at the end other than the knowledge that you are doing this because it's the right thing to do. You will not be congratulated for it. You won't get any ally cookies for it. You won't be celebrated for it. You will have to learn to wean yourself off the addiction to instant gratification and instead develop a consciousness for doing what is right even if nobody ever thanks you for it. Besides, there is no greater reward than being in integrity with your values and living your life in such a way that it makes the world a better place now and for the future.

"Are you sure, sweetheart, that you want to be well?... Just so's you're sure, sweetheart, and ready to be healed, cause wholeness is no trifling matter. A lot of weight when you're well."

—TONI CADE BAMBARA, *THE SALT EATERS*

PART II
the work

week 1

THE BASICS

For our first seven days of this journey, we are going to be diving into what I consider some of the basic foundational aspects of white supremacy. Some of them you have heard of, such as white privilege and white fragility. Others may be new to you, such as white silence and white exceptionalism. Wherever you are in your understanding, I invite you to come to the page with a beginner's mind. Approach each day's topic as if it is your first time, bringing a sense of curiosity and desire to dig deep into the parts of yourself that you are not aware of.

day 1

YOU AND WHITE PRIVILEGE

"I was taught to see racism only in individual
acts of meanness, not in invisible systems
conferring dominance on my group."

—PEGGY MCINTOSH

WHAT IS WHITE PRIVILEGE?

We begin this work today with a term we are most familiar with when
it comes to white supremacy: white privilege. White privilege as a leg-
islative, systemic, and cultural norm has existed for a very long time,
but it was women's studies scholar Peggy McIntosh who first coined
the term *white privilege* in her 1988 paper, "White Privilege and Male
Privilege: A Personal Account of Coming to See Correspondences

Through Work in Women's Studies."* A year later, a substantial portion of that paper was excerpted and published as a paper titled "White Privilege: Unpacking the Invisible Knapsack." The paper contains fifty examples of white privilege. McIntosh writes:

> *I have come to see white privilege as an invisible package of unearned assets that I can count on cashing in each day, but about which I was "meant" to remain oblivious. White privilege is like an invisible weightless knapsack of special provisions, assurances, tools, maps, guides, codebooks, passports, visas, clothes, compass, emergency gear, and blank checks.*[2]

White privilege describes the unearned advantages that are granted because of one's whiteness or ability to "pass" as white. It is very important to note that white privilege is not a concept that is part of the natural order of life. In the absence of white supremacy, white privilege is meaningless.

Following advances in science such as the completion of the Human Genome Project in 2003, scientists were able to examine human ancestry through genetics. Science has proven that the concept of race is not a biological fact but rather a social concept. According to Dr. Harold P. Freeman, who has studied biology and race, "If you ask what percentage of your genes is reflected in your external appearance, the basis by which we talk about race, the answer seems to be in the range of .01 percent. This is a very, very minimal reflection of your genetic makeup."[3]

What we see as observable physical differences among people

---

*   Peggy McIntosh did not learn of David Wellman's use of the term *white privilege* until after she wrote her two essays in 1988 and 1989.

of "different races" are actually just different genotype and phenotype expressions among one race—the human race. Despite our differences in skin color, hair texture, and other physical traits, genetically, you and I are largely the same. However, because race is a deeply held social construct and because of the existence of white supremacy, you and I are not treated the same. You hold white privilege. I do not. And that makes a world of difference. Race *is* a social concept, but that does not make it imaginary when it comes to the very real consequences it has for BIPOC in their daily lives in the presence of white supremacy.

How do we know white privilege is real? There are many who believe that the concept of white privilege is just a liberal idea used to make white people feel bad about themselves. These are people who would argue that in today's world, where things like chattel slavery of African people, race-based discrimination in employment, and race-based school segregation are all illegal, there is no basis for the idea of white privilege. That though white people have had privileges in the past, they no longer do now (with some even arguing that they are the ones who are now the oppressed and marginalized minority group!).

But legal changes in civil rights, though extremely important, do not change the deeply held social construct that there are biologically different races and that one race is superior to the others. And as you will see throughout this book, the belief in this social construct plays out at the unconscious level, affecting thoughts and behaviors that have consequences in both the personal and public realms.

As a young Black girl growing up in the U.K., I was made aware of white privilege at a very early age. I can recall being around seven years old when my mother sat me down to talk about white privilege, or rather my lack of it. She said to me, "Because you are Black, because you are Muslim, and because you are a girl, you are going to have to work three times as hard as everyone else around you to get ahead. You have these three things working against you."

My mother was not talking about my race, religion, and gender being inherently flawed, but rather she was pointing out to me that in a racist and patriarchal society, I would be treated differently. I would not be rewarded the same for the same effort. And she wanted me to know that though this was not fair or right, it was (and still is), sadly, the way things were.

I saw this truth play out at my schools, where I was one of a handful of children of color. Though some of my primary-school teachers understood that they were not supposed to treat me differently from the other children in my class, they still often did, not from a place of malice or intentional racism, but because of their own white supremacist conditioning that unconsciously told them my skin color made me less valuable than my classmates. Though I was usually one of the top students in the class, as well as one of the most well behaved, I often felt overlooked and ignored by my teachers. Though I worked hard to stand out, as my mother had taught me, I often felt invisible to the teacher and less nurtured than the other students (we talk about this more on Day 11). Meanwhile, my white classmates were unconsciously given the privilege of being treated as "normal" and more worthy of the teachers' time, attention, and caring.

It is important to understand that white privilege is separate from but can intersect with class privilege, gender privilege, sexuality privilege, age privilege, able-bodied privilege, or any other type of privilege. So for example, a person can be a woman but still have white privilege. Not having male privilege does not cancel out one's white privilege. A person can lack economic privilege but still have white privilege. Not having wealth does not cancel out white privilege. A person can be gay but still have white privilege. Not having straight privilege does not cancel out white privilege. Lastly, having white privilege does not cancel out one's other marginalized identities, and having white privilege with other privileged identities (e.g., cisgender male, straight, able-bodied, etc.) adds to the amount of overall privilege that you hold.

HOW DOES WHITE PRIVILEGE SHOW UP?

Peggy McIntosh's list of fifty examples of white privilege is a great place to start to see how white privilege shows up. Extracted examples from "White Privilege and Male Privilege" include:

1. I can, if I wish, arrange to be in the company of people of my race most of the time.

7. When I am told about our national heritage or about "civilization," I am shown that people of my color made it what it is.

12. I can go into a book shop and count on finding the writing of my race represented, into a supermarket and find the staple foods that fit with my cultural traditions, into a hairdresser's shop and find someone who can deal with my hair.

15. I did not have to educate our children to be aware of systemic racism for their own daily physical protection.

25. If a traffic cop pulls me over or if the IRS audits my tax return, I can be sure I haven't been singled out because of my race.

36. If my day, week, or year is going badly, I need not ask of each negative episode or situation whether it has racial overtones.

41. I can be sure that if I need legal or medical help, my race will not work against me.[4]

WHY DO YOU NEED TO LOOK AT WHITE PRIVILEGE?

White privilege is the reward that white and white-passing people receive in exchange for participating in the system of white supremacy—whether that participation is voluntary or involuntary. In order to dismantle white supremacy, you must understand how much white privilege is a key aspect of your life, how you benefit (whether knowingly or unknowingly) from your whiteness, what that means for people who do not receive that same benefit, and how you can dismantle it.

You cannot dismantle what you cannot see. You cannot challenge what you do not understand.

People with white privilege often do not want to look directly at their privilege because of what it brings up for them—discomfort, shame, and frustration. But not looking at something does not mean it does not exist. And in fact, it is an expression of white privilege itself to choose *not* to look at it. BIPOC living within white supremacy, however, often do not have this privilege. As a person with white privilege, were you ever told as a child that your whiteness would work against you? That you would have to work harder to compensate for your racial difference? Or was the color of your skin something that was not even discussed because it had nothing to do with what you would be able to accomplish or how you would be treated by the world? That is the essence of white privilege.

Reflective Journaling Prompts

1. In what ways do you hold white privilege? Study the list from Peggy McIntosh and reflect on your own daily life. Make a list of the different ways you hold white privilege in your personal life.

2. What negative experiences has your white privilege protected you from throughout your life?

3. What positive experiences has your white privilege granted you throughout your life (that BIPOC generally do not have)?

4. In what ways have you wielded your white privilege over BIPOC that have done harm (whether or not you intended to do so)?

5. What have you learned about your white privilege that makes you uncomfortable?

day 2

YOU AND WHITE FRAGILITY

> "It is white people's responsibility to be
> less fragile; People of Color don't need
> to twist themselves into knots trying to
> navigate us as painlessly as possible."
>
> —ROBIN DIANGELO

WHAT IS WHITE FRAGILITY?

Today we turn to a phrase coined by author Robin DiAngelo. DiAngelo defines *white fragility* as "a state in which even a minimum amount of racial stress becomes intolerable, triggering a range of defensive moves."[5] It was not until I began directly writing and talking about race that I realized how deeply white fragility runs in the vast majority of white people. In 2017, I published a blog post titled "I Need to Talk to Spiritual White Women about White

Supremacy."[6] The post unexpectedly went rapidly viral to hundreds of thousands of readers around the world, and it elicited reactions of white fragility that ranged widely from the seemingly well-meaning ("This isn't helpful. You're being divisive when you talk about race") to the blatantly vicious ("[insert anti-Black, misogynistic, Islamophobic rant here]"). So many of the white people who were interacting with my work had so little experience talking about race that *any* racial discussion led to them having a total meltdown.

There are two main factors that contribute to the existence of white fragility.

Lack of Exposure to Conversations about Racism

White privilege protects people who are white and white-passing from having to discuss the causes and implications of racism. The privilege of whiteness means that one's day-to-day life is not impacted by skin color, so conversations around racism tend to be shallow and filled with platitudes. Think back over your childhood and young adulthood. Most likely, your racial conversations (if any) were not very nuanced or multilayered. Racism was probably talked about as being something that was binary (e.g., the idea that racists are just mean and bad people) versus an understanding of white privilege and what implications it had for you and BIPOC. This lack of exposure to conversations about race has left you ill-equipped to handle the discomfort of racial conversations as an adult, leading to an inevitable response of white fragility.

Lack of Understanding of What White Supremacy Actually Is

If your understanding of racism and white supremacy does not include a historical and modern-day contextual understanding of colonization, oppression, discrimination, neglect, and marginalization at the systemic level and not just the individual level, then you are going to struggle when it comes to conversations about race. You will assume what is being criticized is your skin color and your individual goodness as a person rather than your complicity in a system of oppression that is designed to benefit you at the expense of BIPOC in ways that you are not even aware of. This lack of understanding leads to white fragility, either by lashing out to defend your individual sense of goodness or feeling that you as an individual are being shamed for being who you are, thus leaving the conversation. This is a dangerous impediment to antiracism.

HOW DOES WHITE FRAGILITY SHOW UP?

Here are a few examples of white fragility in action:

- Getting angry, defensive, or afraid; arguing, believing you are being shamed, crying, or simply falling silent and choosing to check out of the conversation.

- Calling the authorities (the manager, the police, the social media censors) on BIPOC when you are uncomfortable with what they are sharing about race. I have had my social media posts reported and censored more than a dozen times because of white fragility.

- Deleting what you wrote on a social media platform (another form of running away and pretending it never happened), or physically leaving a discussion when you cannot handle where a conversation on racism is going.

In essence, white fragility looks like a white person taking the position of victim when it is in fact that white person who has committed or participated in acts of racial harm.

WHY DO YOU NEED TO LOOK AT WHITE FRAGILITY?

The word *fragile* is so apt, as it describes an inability to withhold even the slightest pressure. Conversations around race and white supremacy are by their very nature uncomfortable. They come loaded with historical and present-day events and experiences that have caused pain, shame, and inequality. White fragility prevents you from having a conversation about racism without falling apart. If you cannot talk about racism, especially about the ways in which you have been unintentionally complicit in racism, then you will never be able to go beyond a mere superficial understanding of racism. This superficial, binary understanding looks like this:

racist people = bad people
not racist people = good people
I want to be a good person, so I cannot be associated with racism.

This desire to be seen as good, by yourself and by others, prevents you from looking at the ways you unknowingly participate in and are a part of white supremacy because of your white privilege. Your desire to be *seen* as good can actually prevent you from *doing* good, because if you do not see yourself as part of the problem, you cannot be part of the solution.

White fragility makes you dangerous to BIPOC. When conversations of racism arise, you jump into defense mode, making you unable to really hear and understand the pain and challenges of BIPOC. The focus becomes to defend the self (and really, one's white privilege and white supremacy as a whole) rather than opening yourself up to an experience of becoming consciously aware of what your privilege has protected you from.

White fragility thus makes you an unreliable ally to BIPOC, because you do not have the resiliency needed to talk about racism. When your BIPOC coworker, friend, or family member shares with you an experience of racism they have been through, you are unable to hear them. You try to convince them they are imagining it or are reading too much into the situation. That they have misunderstood what was said or done—that it was not about race but about something else. Rather than allowing yourself to really hear what they are going through and ask with empathy and compassion how you can support them, you minimize their experiences and let them know, without saying it, that you are not a safe white person for them to be around. As much as you think you have convinced yourself and them with these explanations, all you have really done is make clear your level of white fragility around racial conversations.

Going a step further, white fragility, which is really fear, can quickly turn into active harm. Like going into fight-or-flight mode, your white fragility can cause you to run away, shut down like a deer in headlights, or become more aggressive, violent, and harmful to BIPOC by striking back. In a conversation on racism with a white woman who was a spiritual life coach, she angrily snapped back at me, "Well, what about Black supremacy?" This was a woman who prided herself on being about love and light. But under pressure of being called out for unintentional white supremacy, she struck back. She later came back and apologized, realizing that it was her fragility that she had spoken out from.

Reflective Journaling Prompts

1. How does your white fragility show up during conversations about race? Do you fight, freeze, or flee?

2. Describe your most visceral memory of experiencing white fragility. How old were you? Where were you? What was the conversation about? Why did it bring up white fragility in you? How do you recall feeling during and after the interaction? How do you feel about it today?

3. How have you weaponized your fragility against BIPOC through, for example, calling the authorities, crying, or claiming you're being harmed ("reverse racism!" or "I'm being shamed!" or "I'm being attacked!")?

4. How do you feel when you hear the words *white people*? Do they make you feel uncomfortable?

5. How has your white fragility prevented you, through fear and discomfort, from doing meaningful work around your own personal antiracism to date?

day 3

YOU AND TONE POLICING

"I speak out of direct and particular anger at
an academic conference, and a white woman
says, 'Tell me how you feel but don't say it too
harshly or I cannot hear you.' But is it my
manner that keeps her from hearing, or the
threat of a message that her life may change?"

—AUDRE LORDE

WHAT IS TONE POLICING?

Tone policing is a tactic used by those who have privilege to silence
those who do not by focusing on the tone of what is being said
rather than the actual content. It can be policing BIPOC for using
tones that are "too angry" when talking about racism or celebrating
them over other BIPOC for using tones that are considered more

soft, eloquent, and soothing. In both cases, BIPOC are expected to cater to the white gaze—the white supremacist lens through which people with white privilege see BIPOC—and the comfort level of a person's white fragility when talking about racism.

It is also important to note that tone policing does not only have to be spoken out loud. People with white privilege often tone police BIPOC in their thoughts or behind closed doors, understanding that to do so out loud would be considered racist. However, what exists within can do just as much, if not more, harm than what is spoken out loud. What lies within influences what comes out, whether intentionally or unintentionally.

So much about tone policing has to do with anti-Blackness and racist stereotypes (often intersected with sexism), topics that we will dive deeper into during Week 2 of this book. A white person's expression of anger is often seen as righteous, whereas a Black person's anger is often seen as aggressive and dangerous. Nowhere is this illustrated more clearly than with the on-court and off-court treatment of tennis star Serena Williams. Over the years, Williams has been compared to a gorilla, experienced extra unnecessary drug tests, and had her outfits policed.[7] During her 2018 U.S. Open final match against Naomi Osaka, Williams was called on for a number of violations that confused both her and the crowd. One of these charges was for "verbal abuse" after she called the umpire a "thief." In a *Newsweek* article, Crystal Fleming, an associate professor in sociology and Africana studies at Stony Brook University, writes:

> *Watching the greatest player of all time get tone-policed by a petty man abusing his power was both heartbreaking and infuriating—especially as a black woman... Male players, like James Blake and John McEnroe, have*

come forward to affirm that they have said much worse to
chair umpires without being penalized or fined.[8]

This implicit and explicit bias that Fleming draws our attention to exists not just within professional tennis but also in
homes, at schools and educational institutions, in businesses, in
spiritual spaces, on the internet, and in every space where white
supremacy exists. Tone policing in all these places is the constant judgment—or threat of judgment—on how BIPOC express
themselves. As Claudia Rankine writes, "For Serena, the daily
diminishment is a low flame, a constant drip. Every look, every
comment, every bad call blossoms out of history, through her,
onto you."[9]

Tone policing, or the possibility of it implicitly or explicitly
being used, is a constant drain on the psyches of BIPOC. In an
attempt to avoid the tone policing of people with white privilege,
many BIPOC will often subconsciously preemptively tone police
themselves in order to avoid having to deal with white fragility. As
a writer, it often feels like I'm being pulled in several different directions when trying to express myself. Am I coming across too angry?
Am I coming across too soft? If I use these words, will it provoke
white fragility, and do I have the emotional bandwidth to be able
to deal with that? If I use these words, will they say they prefer me
over other Black women doing antiracism work because they think
I sound "eloquent"? And how do I make it clear that I do not consider that a compliment—that I consider it anti-Black to both me
and other Black women?

It is often a big shock when BIPOC decide they will no longer
tone police themselves and instead fully express their range of
feelings about racism. People with white privilege wonder with

confusion and frustration, *Where is all this anger coming from?*, not realizing it was always there and that the expression of it is the beginnings of self-reclamation as a BIPOC.

HOW DOES TONE POLICING SHOW UP?

Tone policing shows up when people with white privilege say or think the following things to BIPOC during racial conversations. As you consider today's topic, recall if you have ever said or thought these things:

- I wish you would say what you're saying in a nicer way.

- I can't take in what you're telling me about your lived experiences because you sound too angry.

- Your tone is too aggressive.

- The language you are using to talk about your lived experiences is making me feel ashamed.

- The language you are using to talk about your lived experiences is hateful or divisive.

- You should address white people in a more civil way if you want us to join your cause.

- The way you are talking about this issue is not productive.

- If you would just calm down, then maybe I would want to listen to you.

- You are bringing too much negativity into this space, and you should focus on the positive.

There are so many direct and subtle ways that tone policing takes over, and it does not just occur during conversations about race. Tone policing also occurs when you judge BIPOC for not conforming to white norms of communication (e.g., being too loud, using African American Vernacular English, or speaking in ways that do not conform with Standard English).

WHY DO YOU NEED TO LOOK AT TONE POLICING?

Tone policing reinforces white supremacist norms of how BIPOC are "supposed" to show up. It is a way of keeping BIPOC in line and disempowered. When you insist that you will not believe or give credibility or attention to BIPOC until they speak in a tone that suits you, then you uphold the idea that your standards as a white person are more superior. When you control the tone of how BIPOC are supposed to talk about their lived experiences with racism and existing in the world, you are reinforcing the white supremacist ideology that white knows best.

Tone policing is an insidious way of gaslighting BIPOC. Based on the 1938 play *Gaslight*, in which a man dims the gaslights in his home and then persuades his wife that she is imagining the change, gaslighting refers to a form of psychological manipulation that seeks to sow seeds of doubt in a person or persons by making them question their own memory, perception, and sanity.[10] Recall or imagine, if you will, experiencing an act of violence and then being asked to talk about what you experienced without expressing any strong emotions. This is clearly inhumane. To be human is to feel. To talk about pain without expressing pain is to expect a human to recall information like a robot. When you insist that BIPOC talk about their painful experiences with racism without expressing any pain, rage, or grief, you are asking them to dehumanize themselves. Tone policing is both a request that BIPOC share our experiences about racism without sharing any of our (real) emotions about it and for us to exist in ways that do not make white people feel uncomfortable.

When you can understand how you tone police, you can begin to change your behavior so that you can allow BIPOC the full expression of their humanity.

Reflective Journaling Prompts

1. How have you used tone policing out loud to silence, shut down, or dismiss BIPOC? What kinds of words have you used to describe what tone a BIPOC should use?

2. What tone policing thoughts have you harbored inside when you've heard BIPOC talk about race or their lived experiences, even if you didn't say them out loud?

3. How have you derailed conversations about race by focusing on *how* someone said something to you rather than *what* they said to you? Looking back now, why do you think the tone that was being used was more important to you than the content of the information being conveyed?

4. How often have you made your willingness to engage in anti-racism work conditional on people using the "right" tone with you?

5. How have you discounted BIPOC's real pain over racism because the way they talk about it doesn't fit with your world view of how people should talk?

6. How have you discounted BIPOC in general because of the tone they use when they talk?

day 4

YOU AND WHITE SILENCE

> "We will have to repent in this generation
> not merely for the hateful words and
> actions of the bad people but for the
> appalling silence of the good people."
>
> —DR. MARTIN LUTHER KING JR.

WHAT IS WHITE SILENCE?

White silence is exactly what it sounds like. It is when people with white privilege stay complicity silent when it comes to issues of race and white supremacy. Yesterday, we covered tone policing, which is about how you silence BIPOC. Today, we are unpacking white silence, which is about how you stay silent about racism. Both types of silencing arise out of white fragility—a fear of being incapable of talking about race without coming apart. However, white fragility is not the only cause of white silence. White silence is also a defending of the status quo of white supremacy—a manifestation of holding on to one's white privilege through inaction.

As Dr. King points out in this topic's opening quote, it is often the silence of good people that hurts the most. For three years, I was best friends with a white woman whom I adored. We had a lot in common: we were both highly introverted, creative visionaries. Though she lived in the U.K. and I lived in Qatar, we were firmly planted in each other's lives. Each week, we had two-hour accountability calls to catch up, inspire each other, and support each other on our journeys. After a few years of being best friends, we decided that we were going to create and launch a program together. All was moving along smoothly. That is until I was driven to write and publish my viral letter, "I Need to Talk to Spiritual White Women about White Supremacy," and then everything changed.

She fell silent.

I did not realize it at the time, but looking back now, I understand that my words and my work must have triggered her white fragility. She slowly but surely withdrew her presence in my life. Though she saw the public conversations I was having online regarding racism and though she witnessed me experiencing many of the things we talk about in this book, she simply checked out of our friendship. She did not talk to me about my work. She did not ask me how she could support me during this tough time. She did not talk to me about what this work was bringing up for her with regard to her white privilege. She did not say anything. She just fell silent.

And her silence hurt more than any stranger's racial slur thrown at me because it was the betrayal of a person who loved and supported me … as long as I did not talk about racism. When I asked her in a letter before we ended our friendship why she had not shown up to support me over the last few months, she responded that it seemed I had enough support from the other Black women in my life and she did not think I needed her. It was amazing to me that she had shown up to support me without question over the years of our friendship when it came to other experiences in business and in life, but when it came to racism, she did not feel she had anything to contribute. I came to understand that this was a tragic combination of white fragility and white silence that resulted in the end of our friendship.

There are so many BIPOC who have experienced this feeling of betrayal when someone in their life is there for them as long as they do not talk about racism. And if our friends cannot show up for us, what does that mean for how safe we can feel around other people with white privilege?

HOW DOES WHITE SILENCE SHOW UP?

Here are a few examples of white silence in action:

- Staying silent (or making excuses/changing the subject/leaving the room) when your family members or friends make racist jokes or comments.

- Staying silent when you see your colleagues of color being discriminated against at work.

- Staying silent when white people treat your biracial family members in ways they would not treat your white family members.

- Staying silent by choosing not to engage in any conversations about race because of your white fragility.

- Staying silent by not attending protest marches against racism like Black Lives Matter or protests for immigrants at risk.

- Staying silent when your favorite famous spiritual teacher/ coach/mentor/author is called out for racist behavior.

- Staying silent when you witness other white people use their white privilege, white fragility, or tone policing against BIPOC.

- Staying silent by not sharing social media posts about race and racism in your spaces because of the way it might affect your personal or professional life, or simply reposting the posts of BIPOC but not adding your own voice or perspective.

- Staying silent about your antiracism work for fear of losing friends and followers.

- Staying silent by not holding those around you accountable for their racist behavior.

WHY DO YOU NEED TO LOOK AT WHITE SILENCE?

On the surface of it, white silence seems benign. And if not benign, then it could at least be believed to be a stance of neutrality, like the old adage, "If you can't say anything nice, then don't say anything at all." But white silence is anything but neutral. Rather, it is a method of self-protection and therefore also the protection of the dynamics of white supremacy. It protects you, the person with white privilege, from having to deal with the harm of white supremacy. And it protects white supremacy from being challenged, thereby keeping it firmly in place.

Here is a radical idea that I would like you to understand: white silence is violence. It actively protects the system. It says *I am okay with the way things are because they do not negatively affect me and because I enjoy the benefits I receive with white privilege.* When I talk about white silence being violent, I am not just referring to the act of staying silent while observing someone making a racist remark or perpetrating a racist hate crime. Those are the extreme examples that one does not necessarily come across in their day-to-day lives. Remember, white supremacy is not just about individual acts of racism, but rather it is a system of oppression that seeps into and often forms the foundation of many of the regular spaces where you spend your time—school, work, spiritual spaces, health and wellness spaces, and so on. All these spaces are often protected from overt and individual acts of racism while allowing covert and systemic racism to be a part of the accepted culture through white silence.

Here are some ways you use white silence in these spaces. Please note that these ideas will be brought up again and expanded upon more deeply later on in the book.

- In schools and educational institutions, students, parents, educators, and administrators can perpetuate behaviors such as tone policing (implicit or explicit), white saviorism, white superiority, and color blindness against students of color.

- At work, in entrepreneurship, and in corporate spaces, employees and leaders can perpetuate behaviors such as white fragility, cultural appropriation, white centering, and optical allyship.

- In spiritual spaces, seekers, administrators, and leaders can perpetuate behaviors such as white exceptionalism, tone policing, and color blindness.

- In health and wellness spaces, practitioners, medical staff, healers, and teachers can perpetuate behaviors such as anti-Blackness, racist stereotypes, cultural appropriation, and white superiority.

Think about each of these spaces and other spaces where you spend your time. Imagine if each time one of these subtle, covert white supremacist behaviors were not reacted to with white silence but instead responded to by people with white privilege using their voices to challenge the culture and demand change. Now understand that no matter who you are, no matter what level of power, influence, or authority you hold, your voice is needed. Not as a white savior (which we will cover in Week 3), but as someone who recognizes that their privilege can be a weapon used against white supremacy. Your silence is a loud message that you side with white supremacy. The BIPOC around you need to know where you stand and whether they can be safe with you with their experiences.

A quick note for the introverts: Introversion is not an excuse to stay in white silence. As someone who scores pretty highly on the introversion scale, I understand that our natural tendency and preference is to keep to ourselves and to let the extroverts take center stage. However, when it comes to antiracism, leaning on your introversion as a reason why you stay in silence is actually just an excuse to stay in your comfort zone. You can be an introvert and have powerful conversations. You can be an introvert and use writing to disrupt white supremacy. You can be an introvert and show up to protest marches. You do not have to be the loudest voice. But you do need to use your voice.

Reflective Journaling Prompts

1. How have you stayed silent when it comes to race and racism?

2. What types of situations elicit the most white silence from you?

3. How has your silence been complicit in upholding racist behavior?

4. How do you benefit from white silence?

5. Whom in your life do you harm with your white silence?

day 5

YOU AND WHITE SUPERIORITY

"When I got honest with myself, I had to own up
to the fact that I'd bought into the myth of white
superiority, silently and privately, explaining
to myself the pattern of white dominance I
observed as a natural outgrowth of biologically
wired superior white intelligence and ability."

—DEBBY IRVING

WHAT IS WHITE SUPERIORITY?

Merriam-Webster defines *superior* as an adjective meaning "situated
higher up; of higher rank, quality, or importance."[11]

White superiority stems directly from white supremacy's belief
that people with white or white-passing skin are better than and
therefore deserve to dominate over people with brown or black

skin. The most extreme manifestations of this are the KKK, neo-Nazis, and the ideology behind right-wing nationalism. During the writing of this book, I received a hate email from a white man with the subject line "Piss of n*****" that perfectly illustrated the most vile expression of this idea of white superiority. The email read as follows (trigger warning for Black people—this is an extremely racist and anti-Black email):

> *Saracen marxistt sambo malcontents such as yourself are the reason that we are going to have to demonstrate the sacred and eternal truth of white supremacy in a way that will be forever seared into your savage subconscious. Do you have any idea what monkey tribe your slavering ancestors came from? Do you have any notion as to what primitive clicking proto language they spoke or what dark subhuman demons they worshipped? No, you don't, because we took that filth from you and ground it into the dust where it belongs. Imagine what we are going to take from you this time. When the time comes, when the boot is on your neck, you will know why. Understand that you bring this day ever closer with your hate speech. We just wanted to mow our lawns. But we won't stand by as you gear up to eat us like you did in Rhodesia, Congo, Angola, etc. Brace yourself, you impudent uppity n***** whore.*

This email is violent but also clearly ridiculous. And most liberal people with white privilege are not walking around harboring conscious thoughts like that in their minds. These are the kinds of words that reflect the most extreme manifestation of white supremacist ideology. But just because it is extreme does not mean that lighter versions of this ideology do not exist at more unconscious levels for progressive, we-are-all-one-race, peace-loving white people. You do not have to buy into this extreme ideology to harbor thoughts of white superiority. And you do not have to harbor the most extreme manifestations of white superiority in order to cause harm to BIPOC and continue to uphold the system of white supremacy. If we look at this email in the context of today's topic, we can extract ideologies that, while expressed in despicable ways by this man, are also expressed as cultural norms and unconscious beliefs by even the most moderate person with white privilege. For example:

- Words such as *savage*, *monkey*, and *primitive* are what have led to historical and modern-day white saviorism, the myth of the poor Africans who need to be saved by the civilized white people.

- Words such as *hate speech* about my antiracism work have been used against me by some of the most progressive and spiritual white people you will meet, including yoga teachers, life coaches, and spiritual mentors.

- And the sentence on the "dark subhuman demons" my ancestors allegedly worshipped is not too different from modern-day Islamophobia faced by many Muslims such as myself or the institutionalized religious persecution of Native Americans, which took away their freedom to worship in accordance with their traditional religious rites, customs, and ceremonies.

This email is extreme, but it is an extreme manifestation of a widely held and firmly planted dominant paradigm of white supremacy.

The seeds of the idea of white superiority are planted at a very young age, and nowhere is this illustrated more clearly than with the doll tests. In the 1940s, husband and wife team and African American psychologists Drs. Kenneth and Mamie Clark conducted a series of experiments to study the psychological effects of segregation on African American children.[12] Colloquially called the doll tests, the doctors brought together African American children between the ages of three and seven and presented them with four dolls who were identical except for skin color: two black, two white. The children were asked to identify the races of the dolls and which color doll they preferred. A majority of the children preferred the white doll, assigning more positive traits to it than the black doll. The conclusion of the experiment was that "prejudice, discrimination, and segregation" had created a feeling of inferiority among African American children and damaged their self-esteem.

While the 1940s tests showed how inferiority developed in Black children because of white supremacy, it was the updated doll tests in 2010 commissioned by CNN that illustrated how white superiority developed in white children because of white supremacy.[13] Renowned child psychologist and university professor Dr. Margaret Beale Spencer was hired as a consultant by CNN to re-create the doll tests for the modern age. This time, however, white children were tested as well as Black children. The tests showed that white children tended to identify the color of their own skin with more positive attributes and those with darker skins with more negative attributes. The researchers called this phenomenon "white bias." The tests showed that the Black children were far less likely to respond with white bias.

Dr. Spencer concluded, "All kids on the one hand are exposed to the stereotypes. What's really significant here is that white children are learning or maintaining those stereotypes much more strongly than the African American children."

The idea of whiteness being "of higher rank, quality, or importance" begins before you are even consciously aware of it. And because you are unaware of it, it goes largely unchallenged and becomes an internal truth that is deeply held even though it was not intentionally chosen. It is no surprise that around the world today, even in the Middle East, where I live, it is far easier to find white dolls than black or brown dolls in toy shops. White dolls, like white people, are seen as the norm—superior in all ways to black and brown dolls and Black and Brown people.

HOW DOES WHITE SUPERIORITY SHOW UP?

Here are a few examples of white superiority in action:

- Tone policing as described in Day 3's prompt.

- Subscribing to and elevating European standards of beauty (e.g., lighter skin tone, straighter hair). The doll tests illustrated this in horrifying ways, but so does the modern-day lack of representation of dark-skinned and kinky-haired women in film, TV, and media.

- Believing African American Vernacular English (AAVE) is "ghetto" and thinking the correct way to talk is the way you and other white people talk.

- Primarily buying from and working with white entrepreneurs and service providers, whether intentionally or unintentionally.

- Primarily reading books by white authors.

- Primarily learning from and supporting white leaders, whether political or nonpolitical.

- Primarily staying on the "white" side of town.

- Only sharing the work and words of BIPOC if you think it won't offend or upset the other white people in your communities.

- Holding the expectation that BIPOC should "serve" you by providing free emotional labor around racism.

- Believing, in subtle and overt ways, that you are smarter, more valuable, more capable, wiser, more sophisticated, more beautiful, more articulate, more spiritual, and so on, than BIPOC.

WHY DO YOU NEED TO LOOK AT WHITE SUPERIORITY?

Because the idea of your superiority is the very foundation of white supremacy. You continue to perpetuate white supremacy to the extent that you believe in your own and other white people's superiority over BIPOC. Again, it is important to stress that this belief is not necessarily a consciously chosen one. It is a deeply hidden, unconscious aspect of white supremacy that is hardly ever spoken about but practiced in daily life without even thinking about it.

The reality is that you have been conditioned since you were a child to believe in white superiority through the way your history was taught, through the way race was talked about, and through the way students of color were treated differently from you. You have been educated by institutions that have taught white superiority through curricula that favor a white-biased narrative, through the lack of representation of BIPOC, and through the way these institutions handled acts of racism. You have been conditioned by media that continues to reinforce white superiority through an overrepresentation of celebrities and leaders who look like you, through the cultural appropriation of BIPOC fashion, language, and customs, and through the narrative of the white savior. And you likely work within industries that uphold white superiority through a lack of representation of BIPOC at leadership levels, through inclusion and diversity policies that are about optical allyship, and through HR policies (implicit and explicit) that tone police and marginalize employees who are BIPOC.

You need to look at white superiority so that you can begin to unravel it within yourself and dismantle it within the spaces around you.

Reflective Journaling Prompt

1. Think back across your life, from childhood to where you are in your life now. In what ways have you consciously or subconsciously believed that you are better than BIPOC?

_____

Don't hide from this. This is the crux of white supremacy. Own it.

day 6

YOU AND WHITE EXCEPTIONALISM

"White people desperately want to believe that
only the lonely, isolated 'whites only' club
members are racist. This is why the word *racist*
offends 'nice white people' so deeply. It challenges
their self-identification as good people. Sadly,
most white people are more worried about
being called racist than about whether or not
their actions are in fact racist or harmful."

—AUSTIN CHANNING BROWN

WHAT IS WHITE EXCEPTIONALISM?

White exceptionalism is the belief that you, as a person holding
white privilege, are exempt from the effects, benefits, and conditioning of white supremacy and therefore that the work of
antiracism does not really apply to you. I have come to see white

exceptionalism as a double-sided weapon that on one side shields people with white privilege from having to do antiracism work under the belief that "I'm not a racist; I'm one of the good ones" and on the other side shoots out arrows at BIPOC by expecting them to carry the burden of dismantling white supremacy under the belief that racism is something that is a Black or Brown problem but not a white problem.

It is not the right-wing nationalists and overtly proud racists who carry a sense of white exceptionalism. They often wear their true beliefs for all to see. They are clear about who they are, what they stand for, and who they see as a threat. Rather, it is often the white liberals who believe that their progressive ideologies separate them from the racism of the extreme right. It is the people with white privilege who believe that they are not an impediment to antiracism who carry white exceptionalism like a badge of honor.

"They can't mean me. I voted for Obama. I have Black friends. I've had partners who are BIPOC. My kids play with nonwhite kids. I don't even see color! When they talk about racism and white supremacy, they must be talking about those other kinds of white people. Not me. I'm one of the good ones."

Sound familiar? None of these things that you have confidently declared as evidence that you are not racist erases reality. You have been conditioned into a white supremacist ideology, whether you have realized it or not. You are conferred unearned advantages called white privilege, whether you chose it or not. While you experience hardships and oppression in your life from other identities and experiences, you do not experience these things because of your skin color. And your individual acts of voting for a Black president or having relationships with BIPOC do not erase any of this.

HOW DOES WHITE EXCEPTIONALISM SHOW UP?

Some examples of white exceptionalism in action:

* White exceptionalism has shown up every time you saw one of the reflective journaling questions and thought, *I don't do that* or *That doesn't apply to me. I have never or would never think that.*

* White exceptionalism is what convinces you that you don't *really* need to do the work. That you are doing it because it is a commendable thing to do but that you do not have to dig as deep as you are being asked to go.

* White exceptionalism is the little voice that convinces you that you can read this book but you do not have to do the work. That because you have an intellectual understanding of the concepts being presented here, you do not have to diligently write out your responses to questions. That you can just think about it in your mind, and that is enough.

* White exceptionalism is the belief that because you have read antiracism books and articles, listened to social justice–based podcasts, watched documentaries on the effects of racism, and follow some BIPOC activists and teachers, you know it all and do not need to dig deeper.

* White exceptionalism is the idea that you are somehow special, exempt, above this, past this, beyond this thing called white supremacy. That white supremacy is what those other white people do, but not you. It goes hand in hand with white superiority and the belief that you have already done some antiracism

work, you have already shown you're an ally, so you do not need to keep showing up and doing the work.

- White exceptionalism is the hurt "Not all white people!" response when BIPOC talk about white people's behavior.

WHY DO YOU NEED TO LOOK AT WHITE EXCEPTIONALISM?

White exceptionalism is particularly rampant in progressive, liberal, spiritual white people because there is a belief that being these things makes you exempt or above it all. You are not. And the belief that you are makes you dangerous to BIPOC because you cannot see your own complicity and you will not listen when it is being reflected back to you. In his "Letter from a Birmingham Jail," Dr. Martin Luther King Jr. illustrated the dangers of white exceptionalism often found in the group of people he described as the "white moderates":

> First, I must confess that over the past few years I have been gravely disappointed with the white moderate. I have almost reached the regrettable conclusion that the Negro's great stumbling block in his stride toward freedom is not the White Citizen's Council-er or the Ku Klux Klanner, but the white moderate, who is more devoted to "order" than to justice; who prefers a negative peace which is the absence of tension to a positive peace which is the presence of justice; who constantly says: "I agree with you in the goal you seek, but I cannot agree with your methods of direct action"; who paternalistically believes he can set the timetable for

another man's freedom; who lives by a mythical concept
of time and who constantly advises the Negro to wait for
a "more convenient season." Shallow understanding from
people of good will is more frustrating than absolute misun-
derstanding from people of ill will. Lukewarm acceptance
is much more bewildering than outright rejection.[14]

Here is the lesson at the heart of today's topic: If you believe you are exceptional, you will not do the work. If you do not do the work, you will continue to do harm, even if that is not your intention. You are not an exceptional white person, meaning you are not exempt from the conditioning of white supremacy, from the benefits of white privilege, and from the responsibility to keep doing this work for the rest of your life. The moment you begin to think you are exceptional is the moment you begin to relax back into the warm and familiar comfort of white supremacy.

In her essay "Racism—A White Issue," published in the feminist anthology *All the Women Are White, All the Blacks Are Men, But Some of Us Are Brave*, Ellen Pence, a white activist, writes of her realization of her own white exceptionalism. Growing up with a father who was blatantly racist and who preached the natural superiority of whites, she believed that because she did not share this ideology, she was "one of the good ones." In the essay, she writes about attending marches, sending her babysitting money to Martin Luther King Jr., and going to confession to the Black priest at their mainly white parish—taking these as signs that she did not hold the same racist ideology as her father. However, as she became more involved with neighborhood organizing in the program for victims of domestic violence, she began to express some of her own white exceptionalism. She writes, "I watched Blacks and Indians accuse white feminist women of racism.

Certainly, they didn't mean me… I too was oppressed by the white male. So when I heard Women of Color speaking of white privileges, I mentally inserted the word 'male': 'white male privileges.'"[15]

Have you done this? Have you fervently or subconsciously believed that your antiracism actions and/or your other marginalized identities have meant that you are the exception when it comes to white privilege and white supremacy?

Reflective Journaling Prompts

1. In what ways have you believed that you are exceptional, exempt, "one of the good ones," or above the conditioning of white supremacy?

2. In what ways have you acted out of a sense of white exceptionalism when in racial conversations with BIPOC? (For example, when called out for unintentional racist behavior, have you tried to explain or demonstrate that you are "one of the good ones"?)

3. Reread the extract from Martin Luther King Jr.'s letter and think back on the topics we have covered so far in this book. How has your white exceptionalism prevented you from showing up in allyship to BIPOC?

4. Think back to your childhood. How did society (parents, schools, the media) teach you white exceptionalism?

5. If you are a parent, in what ways are you teaching your children white exceptionalism?

day 7

WEEK 1 REVIEW

If you have reached this far in the challenge, you will begin to notice a pattern. All these themes weave in and out of one another, interlocking and interconnecting. That is the sticky web of white supremacy. It is not just the binary black or white of you either *are* a racist or you *aren't*. Rather, it is multilayered behaviors and beliefs that make up a white supremacist worldview. Your internalized beliefs about racism are part and parcel with your view of both the world and yourself. The reflective journaling questions in this book are helping you to become aware of that.

On Day 7, we do not take a day off, because BIPOC do not get to take a day off from (your) white supremacy, but we do reflect. A lot has been brought to the surface over the last six days, and it is important to step back, take stock of what you have learned so far, and integrate so that you can continue on.

If you have been honest with yourself and dug deep for each reflective journal question, then a lot of things should have come to the surface you were not consciously aware of that you are now reflecting on.

On this reflection day, I want to remind you that we are not looking for the happy ending, the teachable moment, or the pretty bow at the end of all the learning. We are also not looking for dramatic admissions of guilt or becoming so frozen with shame that you cannot move forward. The aim of this work is not self-loathing. The aim of this work is truth—seeing it, owning it, and figuring out what to do with it. This is lifelong work. Avoid the shortcuts, and be wary of the easy answers. Avoid the breaking down into white fragility. Question yourself when you think you have finally figured it out— there are always deeper layers, and you will continue to reflect even more as you continue on with this work.

Let's take a moment to go within and recall and find the patterns behind all that you have learned so far about how you perpetuate white supremacy. And then sit in it. Let these understandings work on you and through you.

Reflective Journaling Prompt

1. What have you begun to see and understand about your personal complicity in white supremacy that you were not able to see or understand before you began this work?

week 2

ANTI-BLACKNESS, RACIAL STEREOTYPES, AND CULTURAL APPROPRIATION

In Week 2, we look at color blindness, anti-Blackness, and racist stereotypes.

During the original #MeAndWhiteSupremacy Instagram challenge, I included a content warning for this week asking participants not to share their writings for these particular days on their social media pages so as not to trigger BIPOC in their communities. Over the next seven days, we are going beyond the basics to the real meat of what is traditionally considered racism. We are moving from the benefits and behaviors of whiteness and a more intellectual understanding of white supremacy to what racism against BIPOC looks like in practice. This is going to bring up discomfort, but your discomfort will be small compared to the pain it brings up for BIPOC to hear you "confess" these thoughts, beliefs, and actions. It is important for *you* to bring up these thoughts, beliefs, and actions into your conscious awareness so you have a real understanding of how you perpetuate white supremacy, but the BIPOC do not need to hear these confessions. They are likely already aware of them (since they have always been on the receiving end of them), and to hear them can cause undue emotional pain. Please be as honest as you can with yourself during this week of the work, and keep what you write to yourself or only share with other people with white privilege.

Lastly, if you are a biracial, multiracial, or white-passing Person of Color, please know that this week is particularly heavy. You will likely feel pulled in two different directions during this week—on the one hand, realizing that your white privilege means that you are on the side of the oppressor, and on the other hand, realizing that your non-white racial identity means that you are on the side of the oppressed. During this week, I highly advise being gentle with yourself as you try to navigate these complicated questions while not hiding from their implications. And I would suggest sharing your thoughts and experiences with other people in this work like yourself who are biracial, multiracial, or white-passing People of Color who can best understand and empathize with what this week brings up for you.

day 8

YOU AND COLOR BLINDNESS

> "White people think it is a compliment when
> they do not 'see' you as a black person."
>
> —MORGAN JERKINS, *THIS WILL BE MY UNDOING*

WHAT IS COLOR BLINDNESS?

Race-based color blindness is the idea that you do not "see" color. That you do not notice differences in race. Or if you do, that you do not treat people differently or oppress people based on those differences.

As a child, I could never understand why white parents would shush their children whenever they used the word *Black* to describe a Black person. "Don't say that! It's rude!" they would say in hushed tones, embarrassed that their child had said something that was apparently offensive. But what made it offensive? I *was* Black. This was an observation of difference, not a derogatory judgment. How were they supposed to refer to me? These parents sometimes took it a step further by saying things like, "They're not Black. They're just people." What did this mean? And why was it so important for them to not say the word *Black*? It often left me wondering, was Black synonymous with bad? Was my skin color a source of shame? And if so, was I expected to act as if I were not Black to make white people more comfortable around me?

Young children understand that the idea of "we don't see color" does not make sense. They will not necessarily use the socially constructed terms of race that we as adults use, such as *Black* or *white*, but when asked to describe what color they are and what color their friends are, they use words such as *brown* and *peach* that match up with the colors in their Crayola crayon boxes. When drawing a picture of themselves and their friend who is a different color, they would choose the colors that best match the skin colors they see. So why do we teach children not to see color? More specifically, why is it most often white children and children with white privilege who are taught this idea of color blindness?

When I have asked these questions of white people by pointing out that they do see color, they have often answered back, "I don't mean that I don't literally see color. What I mean is that I treat all people the same, regardless of their color. I mean that I believe that all people should be treated the same, no matter what color they are." They sometimes go on to add, "Talking about different races is so divisive—it creates racism! If we would just stop talking about whites and Blacks and focus on the contents of people's hearts, we wouldn't see any more racism." And herein lie the falsehoods of the promise of racial color blindness.

The promise of the Church of Color Blindness is that if we stop seeing race, then racism goes away. That racism will go away not through awakening consciousness of privilege and racial harm, not through systemic and institutional change, not through addressing imbalances in power, not through making amends for historical and current-day harm, but instead by simply acting as if the social construct of race has no actual consequences—both for those with white privilege and those without it. The belief is that if you act as if you do not see color, you will not do anything racist or benefit from racism. And if you teach your children to not see race too, you can create a new generation of people who will not do anything racist or benefit from racism. Unfortunately, that is not how white supremacy works. The problem does not go away because you refuse to see it. And this kind of thinking is naive at best and dangerous at worst.

In his book *Racism without Racists: Color-Blind Racism and the Persistence of Racial Inequality in Contemporary America*, Puerto Rican author, political sociologist, and sociology professor Eduardo Bonilla-Silva writes about the phenomenon of color-blind racism or what he calls "the new racism." In the opening chapter of his book, he writes:

> *Nowadays, except for members of white supremacist organizations, few whites in the United States claim to be "racist." Most whites assert they "don't see any color, just people"; that although the ugly face of discrimination is still with us, it is no longer the central factor determining minorities' life chances; and, finally, that like Dr. Martin Luther King Jr., they aspire to live in a society where "people are judged by the content of their character, not by the color of their skin."*[16]

Sounds like an admirable outlook to have, doesn't it? The problem is, the philosophy of color blindness does not sufficiently answer the question of why, if there are no racists, racism continues to exist. If white people do not see color, why do BIPOC continue to experience oppression? According to the proponents of color blindness, that is not white people's fault. Bonilla-Silva goes on to explain:

> More poignantly, most whites insist that minorities (especially blacks) are the ones responsible for whatever "race problem" we have in this country. They publicly denounce blacks for "playing the race card," for demanding the maintenance of unnecessary and divisive race-based programs, such as affirmative action, and for crying "racism" whenever they are criticized by whites. Most whites believe that if blacks and other minorities would just stop thinking about the past, work hard, and complain less (particularly about racial discrimination), then Americans of all hues could "all get along."[17]

When it comes to racial color blindness, what begins as a seemingly noble purpose (eradicating racism by going beyond the idea of race) quickly reveals itself as a magic trick designed to absolve people with white privilege from having to own their complicity in upholding white supremacy. Today, notice how color blindness shifts the burden of addressing the consequences of racism onto BIPOC by asking them to stop talking about racism and just work harder and be more like white people. Color blindness is a particularly insidious way for people with white privilege to pretend that their privilege is fictitious.

HOW DOES COLOR BLINDNESS SHOW UP?

Some common statements associated with color blindness:

- I don't see color. I only see people.

- I don't even see you as Black!

- I don't care if a person is black, white, green, yellow, purple, or blue!

- He/she is a Person of Color (when referring to a Black person, because saying *Black* makes the speaker feel uncomfortable).

- I don't know. I don't think that happened because you're Black. I've experienced something like that before, and I'm white (in response to a Black person sharing their lived experience of racism).

- Talking about the races causes racism/racial division.

- Affirmative action is racist.

WHY DO YOU NEED TO LOOK AT COLOR BLINDNESS?

Color blindness causes harm at multiple levels. In the first instance, it is an act of minimization and erasure. When you say "I don't see color" to a BIPOC, you are saying "Who you are does not matter, and I do not see you for who you are. I am choosing to minimize and erase the impact of your skin color, your hair pattern, your accent

or other languages, your cultural practices, and your spiritual traditions as a BIPOC existing within white supremacy."

In the second instance, color blindness is an act of gaslighting. It
is a cruel way of making BIPOC believe that they are just imagining
they are being treated the way they are being treated because of their
skin color, thus keeping them in a position of destabilization and
inferiority. When stopped by airport security for a random check,
BIPOC ask themselves, "Is it really random, or is it because of my
skin color?" When mistreated by a white boss, BIPOC ask themselves, "Is it really because of my behavior, or is it because of my
skin color?" When paid less for a speaking event than their white
counterparts, BIPOC ask themselves, "Is it really because I am less
experienced, or is it because of my skin color?"

Lastly, color blindness is a way to avoid not only looking at other
people's races but looking at your own. So often, white people see
themselves as "raceless" or "normal," with everyone else being a
race or being other, that they fail to investigate how the idea of color
blindness protects them from having to reflect on what it means to
be white in a white supremacist society. When you refuse to look at
color, you refuse to look at yourself as a person with white privilege.

Reflective Journaling Prompts

1. What messages were you taught about color blindness and seeing color growing up?

2. How do you feel when BIPOC talk about race and racism?

3. How have you harmed BIPOC in your life by insisting you do not see color?

4. What is the first instinctual feeling that comes up when you hear the words *white people* or when you have to say *Black people*?

5. What mental gymnastics have you done to avoid seeing your own race (and what those of white privilege have collectively done to BIPOC)?

NOTE ON ANTI-BLACKNESS
FOR DAYS 9–11

> "Because blacks so profoundly symbolize
> race in the white consciousness, any white
> person who wants to challenge racism and
> engage in antiracist practice must work
> to specifically address the messages they
> have internalized about black people."

—ROBIN DIANGELO

Over the next three days, we are going to be looking at anti-Blackness. Before we begin, I want to lay down a basic understanding and definition of anti-Blackness. Merriam-Webster defines *anti-black* as "opposed to or hostile toward black people," and the Movement for Black Lives defines *anti-black racism* as a "term used to specifically describe the unique discrimination, violence and harms imposed on and impacting Black people specifically."[18]

During the live #MeAndWhiteSupremacy Instagram challenge,

Day 9 was one of the first days that really sucked all the air out of the room—both for the participants taking part in the challenge and for me and the other Black women who were observing the work unfolding. Up until this point, we were talking about more foundational aspects of white supremacy and racism. We had not yet talked about the people who were directly affected by racism. I must also admit this was the first day of the challenge that I, as the facilitator of the work, broke down and cried. I say all this to say anti-Blackness is ugly. It hurts. And it is necessary to name it for what it is, for without naming it and confronting it face-to-face, all this work remains an exercise in intellectualizing and theorizing. Antiracism work that does not break the heart open cannot move people toward meaningful change.

Though I use the words *Black women* and *Black men* for Days 9 and 10 and *Black boys* and *Black girls* for Day 11, I invite you to also go beyond the gender binary and reflect on your anti-Blackness toward Black people who are transgender, nonbinary, and gender nonconforming. Black people who identify as LGBTQIA+ and gender nonconforming undoubtedly face even more racial abuse, discrimination, and harm than Black people who identify as cisgender and heterosexual. Finally, please note that when it comes to unpacking anti-Blackness, we are speaking specifically about Black people, not People of Color broadly, but Black people of African descent.

day 9

YOU AND ANTI-BLACKNESS AGAINST BLACK WOMEN

> "Black women know what it means to love
> ourselves in a world that hates us."
>
> —BRITTNEY COOPER, *ELOQUENT RAGE*

WHAT IS ANTI-BLACKNESS AGAINST BLACK WOMEN?

At the end of 2018, Academy, Emmy, and Tony Award–winning actress Viola Davis stepped on stage at the *Hollywood Reporter*'s Women in Entertainment breakfast to accept the Sherry Lansing Leadership Award. During her powerful eleven-minute speech, Davis spoke passionately about what it feels like to be a Black woman in Hollywood:

> *When I started my production company with my hus-*
> *band… we started it because I got tired of always celebrat-*
> *ing movies that didn't have me in it… I don't mean me*
> *Viola, I mean me as a Black woman… I was tired of seeing*

the expansive imagination of writers when they wrote the mess, the joy, the beauty, the femininity of white characters. And maybe an hour into the movie, you saw the obligatory Black character just kind of walking into the camera, who had a name—didn't really have to have a name—because you know nothing about them. And even when you know something about them, it's always so romanticized. We have to be maternal. We have to be the savior. We have to make that white character feel better.[19]

Davis was specifically speaking about the lack of representation and the stereotyping of Black women in movies, but this same attitude exists toward Black women in any medium, any industry, and any community space. Malcolm X famously called Black women the most disrespected, unprotected, and neglected people in America. I believe that attitude toward Black women applies outside America too. Black women bring up all kinds of feelings in people with white privilege and non-Black People of Color: fear, awe, envy, disdain, anger, desire, confusion, pity, jealousy, superiority, and more. Black women are either superhumanized and put on pedestals as queens or the strong Black woman, or they are dehumanized and seen as unworthy of the same care and attention as white women. Both superhumanizing and dehumanizing are harmful because, as Davis rightly points out in her speech, they fail to capture Black women in the mess, joy, beauty, and femininity of women of other races.

Black women are so often underrepresented because they are not seen as women, let alone as people, the same way white women are. Black women are often painted with a broad, monolithic brushstroke that categorizes them into particular stereotypes that rob them of their humanity. In the United States in particular, these stereotypes have arisen out of America's violent slaving history with Black people and Black women in particular. In her book *Sister Citizen: Shame, Stereotypes, and Black Women in America*, author, professor, and political commentator Melissa V. Harris-Perry lays out some of these core stereotypes of African American women, including Mammy, Jezebel, Sapphire, and Strong Black Woman.[20]

These particular stereotype names refer specifically to African-American women and are born from a distorted and violent North American history. However, Black women around the world also experience this white gaze lens of being seen as angry, strong, aggressive, and wild, as well as being believed to be lesser in intelligence and beauty than other women. They are seen as either the aggressive adversary, the sassy sidekick, or the deferent devotee to white women. This perception becomes more exaggerated the more dark-skinned a Black woman is.

In her article "Why Black British Women Understand The Pain Of America's Race Problems", Black British journalist Tobi Oredein writes, "Black women aren't seen as 'ideal' victims due to respectability politics. We're often painted as troublesome, angry and mouthy by images still peddled by the media, TV and film." And in her BBC 4 documentary "Black Girls Don't Cry", Black British television and radio broadcaster Marverine Cole explores how harmful stereotypes of Black women as being strong, sassy, angry and aggressive are contributing to alarming mental health trends among Black women in the U.K. According to a 2014 NHS report, Black British women are more prone to experiencing anxiety, depression, panic and obsessive compulsive disorders than white women.[21]

These boxes do not only constrict Black women's sense of unique individuality and worthiness but they also lead to mistreatment, abuse, and even death. Just one example of this is the proliferation of the U.S. Black maternal health crisis. In 2018, a report by Mothers and Babies: Reducing Risks Through Audits and Confidential Enquiries (MBRRACE U.K.) found that Black women in the U.K. are five times more likely to die in childbirth than white women.[22] According to the CDC, Black women in the United States are three to four times more likely to die from pregnancy-related causes than their white counterparts.[23] When Black women are seen as stronger and less worthy than their white counterparts, it is no wonder that this translates into the medical field. As Harris-Perry writes in *Sister Citizen*, "Therapists are less likely to perceive a black woman as sad; instead they see her as angry or anxious."[24]

As Black women, we even have our own class of misogyny directed at us: misogynoir. A term coined by African American feminist scholar, writer, and activist Moya Bailey, *misogynoir* is defined as "the particular brand of hatred directed at black women in American visual and popular culture."[25] It is a term that describes the place where anti-Black racism and sexism meet, resulting in Black women facing oppression and marginalization under two systems of oppression—white supremacy and patriarchy. Misogynoir reflects the work that law professor, civil rights advocate, and pioneering scholar of critical race theory Kimberlé Crenshaw has led on intersectionality.

HOW DOES ANTI-BLACKNESS AGAINST BLACK WOMEN SHOW UP?

Examples of anti-Blackness against Black women include:

- The derogatory and one-dimensional stereotyping of Black women into categories such as strong, angry, servile, sassy, and so on.

- The underrepresentation of Black women in positions of leadership across industries and community spaces.

- The underrepresentation of Black women in mainstream media as the protagonist.

- The disdain and disregard toward Black women's style and beauty in the past, which has now been replaced by the appropriation of Black women's style and beauty as desirable—as long as they are placed on bodies that are not Black.

- The expectation for Black women to bear the weight of the emotional labor of dismantling white supremacy.

- The expectation from white women that Black women should choose their gender over their race in the feminist movement, disregarding the fact that Black women are both Black and women simultaneously and therefore affected by both sexism and racism at all times.

- Tone policing Black women as too angry or too aggressive to be listened to or believed.

- Idolizing and fetishizing Black women's strength, beauty, and culture.

- Touching Black women's hair without their permission.

- Expecting Black women to fit into very specific stereotypes and roles and then becoming confused and even angry when they do not.

- Being overfamiliar with Black women you do not know in an attempt to create an artificial sense of sisterhood.

- Judging Black mothers as being less capable, kind, or loving than white mothers.

- Desiring praise, comfort, approval, acknowledgment, and recognition from Black women in order to feel good about yourself on your antiracism journey.

- Using Black female friends, partners, and family members as tokens to prove you cannot be racist or harbor anti-Blackness.

- Following a Black woman's leadership only after other white people have shown their approval of that Black woman.

WHY DO YOU NEED TO LOOK AT ANTI-BLACKNESS AGAINST BLACK WOMEN?

It is my belief that the rising and empowerment of Black women is one of the biggest threats to white supremacy. Knowing this, white supremacy works particularly hard to stifle, undermine, marginalize, demonize, and harm Black women.

All anti-Blackness, regardless of who it is directed at, paints Black people as inferior in all ways except the ways that can be used by non-Black people for non-Black gain. When it comes to Black women, this treatment is compounded by the added marginalization faced under sexism. From negative stereotypes that trap Black women in a one-dimensional imagination to the way that Black women's bodies have been treated less like the bodies of human beings and more like the bodies of animals, anti-Blackness against Black women is killing Black women—both physically and psychologically.

How you are in relationships with and to Black women speaks volumes about where you are in your antiracism journey. Do you feel like you cannot relate to Black women? Do you covet Black women's physical attributes yet secretly feel disdain for them as people? Do you assume Black women are less educated, less affluent, and less capable than you? These are just some signs that you harbor anti-Blackness against Black women. This anti-Blackness needs to be excavated, confronted, and owned in order for you to practice antiracism.

Reflective Journaling Prompts

1. Think about the country you live in. What are some of the national racial stereotypes—spoken and unspoken, historic and modern—associated with Black women?

2. What kinds of relationships have you had and do you have with Black women, and how deep are these relationships?

3. How do you think about Black women who are citizens in your country differently from those who are recent immigrants?

4. How have you treated darker-skinned Black women differently from lighter-skinned Black women?

5. What are some of the stereotypes you have thought and negative assumptions you have made about Black women, and how have these affected how you have treated them?

6. How have you expected Black women to serve or soothe you?

7. How have you reacted in the presence of Black women who are unapologetic in their confidence, self-expression, boundaries, and refusal to submit to the white gaze?

8. How have you excluded, discounted, minimized, used, tone policed, or projected your white fragility and white superiority onto Black women?

day 10

YOU AND ANTI-BLACKNESS AGAINST BLACK MEN

"Because white men can't police their
imagination, black men are dying."
—CLAUDIA RANKINE, *CITIZEN: AN AMERICAN LYRIC*

WHAT IS ANTI-BLACKNESS AGAINST BLACK MEN?

In the early 1990s, my father took our family on a trip of a lifetime. We spent a summer holiday sailing around the world on the Danish-owned tanker ship he worked on. My East African father has spent his entire career working at sea as a mariner. Beginning as a young adult, he studied hard and put in the hours, working his way from cadet all the way up to captain.

My father has defied white supremacy's narratives of what he is "supposed" to be. When he told my two younger brothers and me that he was actually the captain of the massive ship, we couldn't believe it. "But Dad," we said, "you can't be the captain! Captains are supposed to be old and have a beard!" He and my mother both laughed. Up until that point, the only captain we had ever seen was Captain Birds Eye, the elderly white man we saw on the television ads for the Birds Eye fish fingers we loved having for lunch. Looking back now, I realize that what I also meant was "You can't be the captain. You're not white."

In my mind, *captain* was a position of high authority and worthy of great respect in the society I lived in, in which I never saw Black men who looked like my father. In refusing to buy into the notion that Black men did not belong in positions of high authority, my father modeled to my brothers and me that no matter what anyone else said, we had the right to be leaders. We had the right to be and do whatever we wanted, wherever we wanted.

Sadly, this is not the message that Black men as a whole receive from white supremacist society. Like Black women, Black men are often trapped in a one-dimensional imagining of what and who they are supposed to be. Nowhere is this more apparent than in the United States where, as with Black women, stereotypes that arise from America's violent history with African people have stripped Black men of their humanity.

The 1915 silent epic movie *Birth of a Nation* portrayed Black men (played by white actors in blackface) as unintelligent and sexually aggressive toward white women—a fabricated propaganda message that was disseminated again and again to justify the violent treatment of Black men as being for the protection of the innocence and purity of white women. A century later, this stereotype of the sexually aggressive Black man still lives on in the collective white psyche, as heartbreakingly witnessed in the tragedy of the wrongly accused Central Park Five who served between six and thirteen years in jail for sexual assault crimes in 1989 they did not commit. During the live #MeAndWhiteSupremacy challenge, one of the phrases that came up again and again about Black men, regardless of where in the world the participant was from, was "I fear Black men."

When Black men's sexuality is not feared, it is often fetishized. Black men are often seen as sexual conquests, there to satisfy the white appetite with their allegedly exaggerated genitalia. They are also sometimes seen as a means to an end—a way to produce biracial babies, a way to feel Black (read: edgier, cooler), or a way to anger white parents who would balk at the thought of their white child being in an intimate relationship with a Black man.

In the United States, there is of course a fraught and abusive relationship between Black men (and Black people) and the justice system. This is enabled in part by white people who are constantly calling the police on Black men (and Black people) for simply existing. A shocking example of this happened in 2018, when two Black men were arrested while quietly sitting at a Starbucks in Philadelphia as they waited to meet a white man for a business meeting. The police were called simply because the two men had not ordered anything (as they were waiting for a friend to show up).[26]

On the big screen, a cinematic trope that film director Spike Lee has expressed frustration toward is that of the *magical negro*—a supporting Black character who comes to the aid of the white protagonist with special insights or mystical powers.[27] Like the American stereotype of the Black woman as Mammy, the magical negro positions Black men as otherworldly but ultimately disposable characters who exist only to selflessly soothe and serve white people.

HOW DOES ANTI-BLACKNESS AGAINST BLACK MEN SHOW UP?

Examples of anti-Blackness against Black men include:

- Stereotyping Black men as sexually aggressive, violent, less intelligent, lazy, and criminal.

- Experiencing surprise when a Black man's behavior, demeanor, or personality does not fit into white supremacist stereotypes.

- Desiring intimate relationships with Black men to shock or surprise white family members or friends.

- Assuming financially successful Black men are either athletes, entertainers, or drug dealers.

- Desiring affinity with or approval from Black men in order to feel more "woke."

WHY DO YOU NEED TO LOOK AT ANTI-BLACKNESS AGAINST BLACK MEN?

Anti-Blackness against Black men upholds the colonialist white supremacist view of Black men as violent, almost animal-like savages and brutes who are less intelligent than their white counterparts and who pose a threat to white womanhood and to society at large. This is dehumanizing. It is easy to blame the past or the criminal justice system for these tropes, but it is important to remember that white supremacy is a system that is upheld by individuals who benefit from it. And it is up to each individual to pull out, confront, and own their part of the narrative that keeps the system running.

When Black men are unconsciously seen in these stereotyped ways, they are limited in both societal consciousness and practice in who and what they can be and where they can be. That quickening of your heartbeat when you see Black men caused by your fears, that excited fetishizing of Black men as sexual conquests, that note of surprise when Black men are tender and multidimensional with their emotions, and all those ideas you have about Black men that negatively differentiate them from white men are clear signs that you harbor anti-Blackness against Black men. Dig it out today and get to the core of it so you can stop trapping Black men in a white supremacist story of your own making.

Reflective Journaling Prompts

1. Think about the country you live in. What are some of the national racial stereotypes—spoken and unspoken, historic and modern—associated with Black men?

2. How do you think about Black men who are citizens in your country differently from those who are recent immigrants?

3. What kinds of relationships have you had and do you have with Black men, and how deep are these relationships?

4. How have you treated darker-skinned Black men differently from lighter-skinned Black men?

5. What are some of the stereotypes you have thought and negative assumptions you have made about Black men, and how have they affected how you have treated them?

6. How have you excluded, discounted, minimized, used, tone policed, or projected your white fragility and white superiority onto Black men?

7. How have you fetishized Black men?

8. How much freedom do you give Black men in your mind to be complex and multilayered human beings?

day 11

YOU AND ANTI-BLACKNESS AGAINST BLACK CHILDREN

> "Black people love their children with a
> kind of obsession. You are all we have,
> and you come to us endangered."
>
> —TA-NEHISI COATES, *BETWEEN THE WORLD AND ME*

WHAT IS ANTI-BLACKNESS AGAINST BLACK CHILDREN?

The Black women and Black men we talked about in Days 9 and 10 all started off as Black children. Black children in the white imagination often start out as cute. Cute brown faces with cute curly hair. And then at some point, they grow up, and in the white imagination, they are suddenly not so cute anymore.

As a young child, I often wondered why my mother worked so hard for us to excel at school. She didn't just want us to do well; she wanted us to outshine every other student in our class. Lucky for me, I have always been an avid learner. But the pressure to always be at the top of the class was tough. As an adult looking back, I can see how daunting it must have been raising Black Muslim children in a society that was anti-Black, especially as a Black mother raising children alone while my father worked at sea many months of the year. We were in a society that treated Black people and immigrants as if we were less intelligent, less civilized, and less worthy of accomplishment and success than everyone else. My mother often tells us about our childhood, "I wanted you to be the best!" My parents have both always strived for excellence, but when I think back on my mother's words, I also think that what she meant is that she did not want any white person to have any reason to pigeonhole us. She did not want them to limit us to what they saw Black people as being capable and worthy of. She wanted to bulletproof and supercharge us, knowing full well how white supremacy treats Black children.

Two recent U.S. studies show how Black children experience "adultification," the experience of being seen and treated as though they are older than they actually are. In 2014, Professor Philip Goff and colleagues published an experimental study called "The Essence of Innocence: Consequences of Dehumanizing Black Children." The findings of the study were that "Black boys are seen as older and less innocent and that they prompt a less essential conception of childhood than do their White same-age peers. Further, our findings demonstrate that the Black/ape association predicted actual racial disparities in police violence toward children."[28] In other words, the study showed that from the age of ten, Black boys are perceived as older and more likely to be guilty than their white peers and that police violence against them is more justified. We have only to look at Black boys like Tamir Rice and Trayvon Martin who were killed because they were not seen as children but feared as Black men who could do harm to anyone at any moment.

In 2017, a groundbreaking U.S. study titled "Girlhood Interrupted: The Erasure of Black Girls' Childhood" was published by the Georgetown Law Center on Poverty and Inequality. The study provided—for the first time—data showing that adults view Black girls as less innocent and more adult-like than their white peers, especially in the age range of five to fourteen. Specifically, the study found that, compared to white girls of the same age, it was perceived that:

- Black girls need less nurturing.
- Black girls need less protection.
- Black girls need to be supported less.
- Black girls need to be comforted less.
- Black girls are more independent.
- Black girls know more about adult topics.
- Black girls know more about sex.[29]

With regard to the treatment of Black girls in the education system, the study suggests that "the perception of Black girls as less innocent may contribute to harsher punishment by educators and school resource officers. Furthermore, the view that Black girls need less nurturing, protection, and support and are more independent may translate into fewer leadership and mentorship opportunities in schools." And with regard to the treatment of Black girls in the juvenile system, the study suggests that "the perception of Black girls as less innocent and more adult-like may contribute to more punitive exercise of discretion by those in positions of authority, greater use of force, and harsher penalties."[30]

Anti-Blackness and the adultification of Black children results in Black children not being treated as children but rather as the adult Black people they will grow up to be in the white imagination. Black children are superhumanized as if they do not experience the same kind of pain, fear, and trauma as white children do and dehumanized as if they are not worthy of the same level of care and attention that white children are.

As an example, in 2015, then fifteen-year-old Dajerria Becton was dragged by her hair, slammed to the ground, pinned, and handcuffed by a white male police officer while she cried out for her mother outside a pool party she was attending.[31]

Black children are also often pitied in the white imagination, with white people wanting to "save" them, whether from their own Blackness, from their Black parents (who are seen through the white gaze as being inferior in their ability to parent as compared to white parents), or in the case of white saviorism in Africa, from the plight of being "poor Africans." All this, however, is often just another way for white people to affirm themselves as good. It does not take into account what the children actually need but focuses on white people's twisted imaginings of Black people.

HOW DOES ANTI-BLACKNESS AGAINST BLACK CHILDREN SHOW UP?

Examples of anti-Blackness against Black children include:

- Fetishizing about wanting to birth or adopt Black children.

- Pitying Black children.

- Wanting to "save" Black children.

- Using Black children as props (e.g., traveling on mission trips to Africa to take pictures with African children).

- The adultification of Black children (treating them as older and less innocent than their white counterparts).

- Overlooking Black children.

- Expecting Black children to be stronger than their white counterparts.

- Expecting Black children to be less intelligent than their white counterparts.

- Using Black children to prove that you or your children are not racist by being overly nice to them or wanting your children to be friends with them (this is a form of tokenization).

WHY DO YOU NEED TO LOOK AT ANTI-BLACKNESS AGAINST BLACK CHILDREN?

Anti-Blackness toward Black people does not begin when they are adults. It begins when they are children. From an early age, Black children are treated with less care and more suspicion than their white counterparts, meaning that, throughout their lives, Black people are treated as inferior and worthy of racism—both in thought and action. Looking at your relationship with Black children is very uncomfortable. After all, children are innocent. However, the truth is that some children are treated as less innocent than other children. If you really want to get to the root of your anti-Blackness, then you have to start at the beginning. Black children are not exempt from your anti-Blackness. You have a responsibility to look at this head-on today so that you can root it out within you and understand how your unconscious anti-Blackness toward Black children contributes to a socially accepted way of treated Black children and Black people as if they are less than.

Reflective Journaling Prompts

1. Think about the country you live in. What are some of the national racial stereotypes—spoken and unspoken, historic and modern—associated with Black children?

2. How do you think about Black children who are citizens in your country differently from those who are recent immigrants?

3. How have you viewed or do you view Black children when they are young versus when they get to their teens and young adulthood?

4. How have you treated Black children differently from white children? And how have you treated darker-skinned Black children differently from lighter-skinned Black children?

5. How have you tokenized and fetishized "cute Black kids" or "cute mixed kids"?

6. How have you wanted to "save" Black children?

7. If you are a white or biracial parent of Black children, what anti-racism work have you been doing on yourself and in your communities to make the world a safe space for your children? Do you protect your kids when someone others your Black children, or do you retreat into white silence?

day 12

YOU AND RACIST STEREOTYPES

"We them barbarians
Beautiful and scaring them
Earth shakin' rattling
Be wild out loud again"

—MONA HAYDAR

WHAT ARE RACIST STEREOTYPES?

Though we have spent the last few days looking at anti-Blackness,
white supremacy has not just hurt and killed Black people. It has
also hurt and killed Indigenous people and People of Color (POC)
from countries around the world. And just like there are racist
stereotypes about Black people, there are also just as damaging
stereotypes about other groups of people who are not white. The

enforcement of racist stereotypes in the media and in the collective subconscious is the way in which white supremacy continues to maintain nonwhite people as the "other," the ones who should be feared, ridiculed, marginalized, criminalized, and dehumanized. Racist stereotypes within white supremacy emphasize again and again that those who are not "like us" are different and therefore a threat.

Before we go deeper into today's prompt, it is important for me to pause here and offer a clarification on the difference between prejudice and racism.

All people, regardless of race, can hold some level of prejudice toward people who are not the same race as them. A person of any race can *prejudge* a person of any other race based on negative racial stereotypes and other factors. Prejudice is wrong, but it is not the same as racism. Racism is the coupling of *prejudice* with *power*, where the dominant racial group (which in a white supremacist society is people with white privilege) is able to dominate over all other racial groups and negatively affect those racial groups at all levels—personally, systemically, and institutionally.

Therefore, though a BIPOC can hold prejudice against a white person, they cannot be racist toward a white person. They do not have the *power* (which comes with white privilege) and the backing of a *system of oppression* (called white supremacy) to be able to turn that prejudice into domination and punishment in a way that a white person would be able to if the tables were reversed.

The acronyms BIPOC or POC can be helpful linguistically in conveying the idea that we are referring to people who do not hold white privilege, but what we gain in terms of ease of communicating we lose in terms of conveying the nuanced experiences that these different racial groups have when it comes to their experiences with white supremacy. When we say BIPOC or POC, we are essentially clumping people from all kinds of different cultures and racial experiences into one clumsily assembled group. This flattens their experiences and gives the impression that they all experience white supremacy in the same way, which they do not.

The reason why I specifically chose to cover anti-Blackness separately from Indigenous people and POC is because Black people also experience anti-Blackness from these groups. However, just because Indigenous people and non-Black POC can hold anti-Blackness feelings does not mean they do not have their own fraught and abusive experiences with white supremacy. For that reason, during this day of the work, I invite you to break down the acronym POC more deeply, because different racial groups experience white supremacy in different ways, and even with these more broken down groupings of countries, racism is experienced differently.

For example, in the group of people broadly called Asians, white supremacy impacts them in different ways depending on whether they are South Asian, East Asian, or Southeast Asian, as each subgroup has different racist stereotypes that it has to contend with.

Here are some of the broad groups to think about for this day's journaling:[32]

- Asian people
- Latinx people
- Indigenous people
- Arab people
- Biracial and multiracial people

A few things to keep in mind as you look at racist stereotypes with these groups:

- Each group in this list covers many countries and nations, each with its own rich and complex history—both with white supremacy/colonialism and with one another. Notice any desire to want to treat each group as one flattened group rather than different countries. Remember that white supremacy's aim is to collapse all racial "others" into one group to dominate and marginalize.

- Religions are not races. However, racial groups often experience religious prejudice and discrimination associated with certain racial groups, regardless of whether they observe that particular religion or even belong to that particular religion. So for example, though Arab is not synonymous with Muslim, non-Muslim Arabs can experience Islamophobic-type stereotypes because of the media-driven idea that all Muslims are Arab.

- You can belong to a group that experiences prejudice stereotypes and oppression while still holding white privilege or white-passing privilege. One does not cancel out the other but rather reminds us that it is both/and, not either/or.

- Colorism is also very important to keep in mind. Darker-skinned people often experience more racism than lighter-skinned people.

- Just because a stereotype seems positive does not mean it is not harmful. Stereotypes rob people of their complex individuality and erase the impact that colonization has had on why some of these stereotypes have emerged.

HOW DO RACIST STEREOTYPES SHOW UP?

Racist stereotypes differ depending on the racial group. Here are some examples of racist stereotype words sometimes associated with different groups (note that these differ from group to group and also across gender):

- Poor
- Lazy
- Less educated
- Less intelligent
- Exotic
- Spicy
- Spiritual
- Sexist
- Oppressed
- Terrorists

- Drug dealers
- Domineering
- Effeminate
- Aggressive
- Demure
- Alcoholics
- Overachieving
- Helpless
- Opportunists

WHY DO YOU NEED TO LOOK AT RACIST STEREOTYPES?

Racist stereotypes continue to reinforce the idea that those who do not hold white privilege should not be given that privilege because they are other, inferior, and a threat to white civilization.

Racist stereotypes are used by politicians, policy makers, and the media to justify why certain groups of people should be treated the way that they are. It is easy to blame those in positions of leadership who drive racist stereotype narratives. But what about the narratives you are holding that continue to make it acceptable to allow people from other races to be talked about and treated the way they are?

Although they are ridiculous when said out loud, racist stereotypes fester internally as subtle, dangerous, and logical-seeming reasons that explain why racism is justified. Though you would never say or consciously believe these stereotypes out loud, they do live inside you. And when coupled with the power you hold as someone with white privilege, these prejudices give you the ability to enforce white supremacy.

If subconsciously, you believe that Indigenous people are primitive, or Arabs are terrorists, or Latinx people are drug dealers, then at some level, it makes sense to you when you see it reflected back to you through media messages. And therefore, at some level, it makes sense to you that they face the kind of treatment they face by the educational system, the justice system, the health-care system, the immigration system, the employment sector, and so on. Uncovering your racist stereotypes will help you to see how you actively contribute to white supremacy by believing white supremacy's lies about the inferiority of those who do not look like you.

Reflective Journaling Prompts

What have you learned about you and racist stereotypes? Begin by making a list of the different racial groups of people found in your country. Where possible, break these down into countries.

1. What are some of the national racial stereotypes in your country—spoken and unspoken, historic and modern—associated with Indigenous people and non-Black POC?

2. What are the racist stereotypes, beliefs, and thoughts you hold about the different racial groups of people? In what ways do you paint them all with one brush rather than seeing them as complex individuals?

3. How do you think about POC who are citizens in your country differently from those who are recent immigrants? How do you think about those who are more assimilated versus those who are less assimilated (e.g., if they practice your country's social norms, if they have accents that sound like yours, etc.)?

4. How do you think about and treat Indigenous children and non-Black children of color differently from white children?

5. How do you think about and treat darker-skinned Indigenous people and POC differently from those who are lighter-skinned?

6. In what ways have you superhumanized parts of the identities of Indigenous people and POC while dehumanizing other parts?

day 13

YOU AND CULTURAL APPROPRIATION

> "When you're a member of the privileged
> group, you don't take kindly to someone
> telling you that you can't do something."
>
> —TIM WISE, *WHITE LIKE ME*

WHAT IS CULTURAL APPROPRIATION?

Over the past five days, you have been looking at the specific ways in which you have unconsciously perpetuated the dehumanization of BIPOC, whether through thought or action, through color blindness, anti-Blackness, and racial stereotypes. By today, you have probably begun to realize that white supremacy is usually present in some form when you are interacting with someone who does not hold white privilege. There is always a hierarchical power and privilege dynamic at play. At the top of that hierarchy are those with white privilege, holding a position of institutional and psychological superiority. And at the bottom of the hierarchy are those without white privilege, holding a position of institutional and psychological inferiority. This dynamic coupled with violent force is what made slavery and colonization possible.

Talking about cultural appropriation in today's modern and globalized world is always tricky. For one thing, because of advancements in travel, technology, and the widespread use of the internet, we are more culturally connected with one another than we have ever been before. This elicits the questions how do we define what culture is, how is it now formed, and who "owns" what?

Cultural appropriation can include the appropriation of another culture's objects, motifs, symbols, rituals, artifacts, and other cultural elements. However, one person from one racial group can think something is culturally appropriative while another person from that same group disagrees and considers it cultural appreciation or cultural exchange. It is factors like these that make it difficult to classify what cultural appropriation is, and this is why I avoid making definitive lists of what is and is not cultural appropriation. That all said, we must still talk about it, because it is a facet of white supremacy.

In her book *So You Want to Talk about Race*, author Ijeoma Oluo broadly defines *cultural appropriation* as "the adoption or exploitation of another culture by a more dominant culture."[33] The first and most important thing we need to understand therefore about cultural appropriation is that it occurs between a *dominant* and a *nondominant* or *marginalized* culture. To clarify, what makes one culture dominant and another nondominant has nothing to do with the specifics of the countries where those cultures are from (e.g., population size, national GDP, or how far back that culture's history goes), but rather it is about the historic and present-day relationship that exists between the two cultures. We must ask ourselves whether that relationship includes colonization, land theft, mass kidnapping and enslavement, attempted genocide, forced assimilation, segregation, legalized racial discrimination, and the reinforcement of negative racist stereotypes. If so, then the culture that has benefited from this oppression is identified as the dominant one, and the culture that has suffered from this oppression is identified as the nondominant one. When considering cultural appropriation in the context of white supremacy and BIPOC, it is clear to see that those who hold white privilege always belong to the dominant culture.

I know what you might be thinking. "Okay, but all that stuff was in the past! And besides, isn't cultural sharing a way to *solve* racism?"

These arguments, though attractive, are fundamentally flawed. Let us consider what we have covered so far in this work:

- **Color blindness:** Though biologically, we are all one race, the consequences of the social construct of race are still very real. The argument that we should act like one giant human culture who share everything equally would work if not for racism and the existence of privilege. The argument of "that stuff was in the past" attempts to create a fictional postracial present that does not reflect our current reality. We cannot just pretend away the lived experiences of BIPOC under white supremacy. And we cannot pretend that one culture that has always held a position of dominance and privilege is now magically color-blind and in an egalitarian relationship with BIPOC cultures.

- **Anti-Blackness:** Anti-Blackness is most definitely not a thing of the past, and it continues to marginalize and harm Black people around the world to this day.

- **Racist stereotypes:** Racist stereotypes continue to abound in the media and in people's minds, causing marginalization, loss of opportunities, erasure, suspicion, and ridicule. Again, this is not a thing of the past. Further, the impacts of racist history are still present today. Disparities and discrimination that were initiated by historical chapters in time still exist today.

So when we consider history and the present day, it becomes clear that it is very hard to appreciate or exchange from a culture that your culture has historically oppressed and toward which you personally hold thoughts of superiority. The idea that you can appreciate rather than appropriate from a culture that you see as less than you is highly doubtful. Often times, what you describe as cultural appreciation is a form of tokenizing and exoticizing while continuing to discard and dehumanize the actual people of that culture. Often times, the cultural elements that are appropriated are stripped of their original cultural context, meaning, and significance and used in such a way as to serve or pleasure whiteness.

Does that mean that you should not get to share or use any elements from any other culture except your own? I think this is the wrong question to ask because it can only produce a binary yes or no answer, and we do not live in a binary world. There are ways to appreciate other cultures that are respectful and honoring, and that begins with asking deeper questions like:

What is the history that exists between my culture and that culture?
What are some of the subconscious negative stereotypes and racist
beliefs I have toward people of that culture?
What are ways that I can financially compensate people from the
culture I am purchasing cultural elements from?

*In what ways am I supporting, protecting, and uplifting people
 from that culture in my community?*

*Do I understand the historic significance and sacredness of this
 cultural element to that culture?*

Does something like this cultural element exist in my own culture?

*Why is it so important to me to partake in this cultural element at
 the risk of offending people from that culture?*

*Are there ways for me to partake in this cultural element without
 financially benefiting from it in ways that people from that
 culture would not?*

*If I am financially benefiting, are there ways in which I can redirect
 some of that financial benefit toward the people of that culture?*

*Knowing what I now know about me and white supremacy, how
 good does it feel to partake in this cultural element the way I
 have been doing so far? Does something need to change, and if
 so, what?*

HOW DOES CULTURAL APPROPRIATION SHOW UP?

Cultural appropriation shows up in a number of different spheres,
including but not limited to:

- **Fashion:** the appropriation of cultural fashion styles, usually by
  white designers appropriating from BIPOC, and often without
  credit or attribution to the original culture; the use of blackface
  symbology.

- **Hair:** the appropriation of traditionally African heritage hair-
  styles worn on non-Black people.

- **Beauty:** the appropriation of BIPOC physical attributes (e.g., thicker lips, rounder hips and thighs, or darker skin, whether through tanning or Blackfishing).

- **Spirituality:** the appropriation of sacred BIPOC spiritual cere-monies, rituals, iconography, practices, and objects.

- **Wellness:** the appropriation of BIPOC traditional wellness practices and healing modalities.

- **Music:** the appropriation of Black music styles, often filtered through a white lens (e.g., rap music).

- **Cultural holidays and events:** cultural holidays and events that perpetuate appropriative practices, such as Halloween costumes or the use of the blackface character Zwarte Piet or Black Pete in the Netherlands for the annual celebration of Sinterklaasavond (St. Nicholas's Eve).

- **Linguistic styles:** the appropriation of AAVE by non-Black people.

WHY DO YOU NEED TO LOOK AT CULTURAL APPROPRIATION?

What makes acts of cultural appropriation harmful is not the desire to share in a culture different from yours. Rather, it is the power dynamic between the dominant and nondominant cultures. Often, the appropriation is accompanied by an erasure of the nondominant culture's origin story of that practice, while the dominant culture is able to profit—whether financially or socially—by the act of appropriation. What is seen as inferior, uncivilized, less advanced, savage, or ugly when owned by the nondominant culture is suddenly seen as superior, advanced, cultured, and beautiful when used by the dominant culture. For example, when white people use AAVE, they are perceived as more woke or cool. When Black people use AAVE, they are seen as ghetto and less educated.

Cultural appropriation upholds the white supremacist ideology that white people can take what they pick and choose from Black and Brown people without consequence and that when a person with white privilege adopts something from a Black or Brown culture, they are somehow enhanced because they have adopted something "exotic." Cultural appropriation is collecting the parts of Blackness and Brownness that appeal to whiteness while discarding actual Black and Brown people.

Lastly, cultural appropriation rewrites history with whiteness at the center. So for example, though yoga has its roots in India as a spiritual practice, it is now seen as a predominantly white-centered practice that is focused largely on physical health. When we think of a yoga teacher, we think of a white person. While Native Americans were historically prohibited from practicing their religious practices by laws and government policies, now white New Age spirituality co-opts and financially profits off these practices, sacred tools, ritual plants, and ceremonial items. Black styles of hair have been vilified as being less beautiful (when worn by Black people), but now the predominantly white fashion world, which has historically neglected the care of Black hair, co-opts Black hair styles like braids, cornrows, and Bantu knots, calling them "edgy" and "urban."

What white supremacy once denied to and vilified in entire

races of people it has discriminated against, it now appropriates and commodifies. This is racism, and it must be wrestled with.

Reflective Journaling Prompts

1. How have you or do you appropriate from nonwhite cultures?

2. What actions have you taken when you have seen other white people culturally appropriating? Have you called it out? Or have you used your white silence?

3. Have you been called out for cultural appropriation? How did you respond?

4. How have you profited (socially or financially) from cultural appropriation?

5. How have you excused cultural appropriation as being "not that bad"? How do you feel about it now having done thirteen days of this work?

day 14

WEEK 2 REVIEW

This week of the work was heavy. Ugly. You have probably had multiple thoughts of running away and forgetting you had ever heard of me or this work. But you are here anyway, because you are starting to understand what the *real* work is. And once you begin to see it, you cannot unsee it.

During Week 1 of this work, we looked at what I call the basics, some of the behaviors that lay the foundation for white supremacy–style thinking. During this second week, we faced the ugly beast of how white supremacy manifests through the myth of color blindness and the racism of anti-Blackness, stereotypes, and cultural appropriation. Without doing the foundational work at Week 1, you could not have faced Week 2 without really digging in. It is easy to see how white privilege, white fragility, tone policing, white silence, white superiority, and white exceptionalism lead to the thoughts and behaviors we have covered in Week 2.

White supremacy, therefore, is not a simple litmus test of whom you vote for or what relationships you have with BIPOC, but rather, it is a set of subtle behaviors, thoughts, and beliefs, often unconscious, that when put together make up a really scary jigsaw puzzle. It is not enough to look at just one or two pieces of the jigsaw. To see the whole picture, we have to look at each piece in turn and see the entire story being told.

Reflective Journaling Prompts

1. What have you begun to see that you cannot unsee?

2. What have you begun to unearth about yourself when it comes to white supremacy?

3. What have these last thirteen days (and especially the last six days) shown you about how white supremacy works through you?

4. What have you learned about the dehumanizing ways you think about and treat BIPOC and why?

5. What have you learned about you and anti-Blackness?

6. If you are biracial, multiracial, or a Person of Color holding white privilege, what has this week brought up for you? How can you find grounding and self-care for yourself after this heavy week?

7. If you came to this book thinking you were "one of the good white people" or an ally to BIPOC, how do you feel about that now?

8. How are you thinking differently about your white privilege, white fragility, white tone policing, white silence, white superiority, and white exceptionalism now?

week 3

ALLYSHIP

In Week 3, we look at the concept of allyship and the behaviors, thoughts, and actions that often contort what this term means. We begin the week with white apathy, something you may be feeling after fourteen days of this work. We then go on to look at some of the behaviors that get in the way of the practice of antiracist allyship.

Before we dive into this week, let's create some clarity around what we mean when we talk about allyship. A definition of *allyship* that really resonates for me is this one by PeerNetBC. They define allyship as "an active, consistent, and challenging practice of unlearning and reevaluating, in which a person of privilege seeks to work in solidarity with a marginalized group. Allyship is not an identity—it is a lifelong process of building relationships based on trust, consistency, and accountability with marginalized individuals and/or groups. Allyship is not self-defined—our work and our efforts must be recognized by the people we seek to ally ourselves with."[34]

The first thing to understand is that allyship is not an identity but a practice. A person with white privilege does not get to proclaim themselves an ally to BIPOC but rather seeks to practice allyship consistently. And a person with white privilege does not get to be the judge of whether what they are practicing actually is allyship, because what they might deem to be allyship could actually be white centering, tokenism, white saviorism, or optical allyship instead. The intention of this week of the work is to help you to better understand how you are showing up (or not showing up) in allyship and to help you become more aware of the ways in which you are doing more harm than good despite your best intentions.

day 15

YOU AND WHITE APATHY

"Our humanity is worth a little discomfort,
it's actually worth a *lot* of discomfort."

—IJEOMA OLUO

WHAT IS WHITE APATHY?

Merriam-Webster defines *apathy* as "lack of feeling or emotion; lack of interest or concern" and gives the synonyms "indifference, unconcern, passivity, detachment, insensitivity, dispassion, disregard."[35]

White apathy arises as a self-preservation response to protect yourself from having to face your complicity in the oppression that is white supremacy. But like white silence, white apathy is not neutral. It is easy to judge intentional and planned-out acts of racism as the only manifestation of white supremacy. However, the intentional nonaction of white apathy is just as dangerous as these intentional actions of racism.

White apathy lacks aggression, but it is deadly in its passivity. Through detachment and indifference to racial harm, white apathy says, "It's really sad that this is happening, but it's not my problem." White apathy therefore tries to enforce this idea that white supremacy is a problem inherent to BIPOC and not a problem created and maintained by people with white privilege. White apathy says to BIPOC, "I wish I could help with your cause. But unfortunately, I'm just too busy right now. Unfortunately, I'm just too tired right now. Unfortunately, it's just not a priority for me right now. Maybe when I can clear a bit more space for myself, I can make some time to come help you out. Until then, all the best."

But dismantling white supremacy is not a charitable cause. It is not a social media awareness campaign or a fund-raising Kickstarter. It is a system of oppression that confers unearned advantages and privileges to one group of people at the expense of other groups of people. It is an ideology that perpetuates harm through discrimination, abuse, racist stereotypes, and criminalization. If people with white privilege feel a sense of apathy about dismantling this system, imagine how BIPOC feel about having to face it down every day.

White apathy is the choice to stay in the warm and safe comfort of white supremacy and the privileges it affords.

There are several factors that we have covered in this book so far that contribute to white apathy:

White Privilege

The privilege of whiteness means not having to deal with white supremacy if one chooses not to. After all, white supremacy benefits those who are white or white-passing in ways that are very attractive. White apathy says, "Why throw that away? There is so much more to lose than there is to gain."

White Fragility

White fragility causes so much discomfort that it is easy to decide that it is not worth it and return to the comfort of white supremacy. White apathy is like a warm blanket that says, "This is too hard. Let's go back to sleep."

White Silence

White silence and white apathy go hand in hand, feeding into each other. You are silent because you are apathetic to racism, and your apathy feeds even more silence.

White Exceptionalism

The idea that "I'm one of the good ones" puts you in a mindset that you are not racist and therefore you do not have to do anything more to practice antiracism. Exceptionalism gives you a false sense of pride that is really white apathy in disguise.

Color Blindness

If you believe that we are in a postracial time in history, then you feel no urgency to practice antiracism. In fact, it is easy to convince yourself that your choice to "not see color" makes you antiracist and therefore there is no further work to be done. You practice white apathy while convincing yourself you are practicing antiracism.

Anti-Blackness and Racist Stereotypes

These deeply held subconscious thoughts create a belief that at some level, BIPOC deserve the treatment they are facing because they are inferior, lazy, ugly, dangerous, uncivilized, unworthy, and so on. Apathy here says, "I wish racism was not a reality, but

BIPOC kind of bring it upon themselves because of who they are." This kind of justification is bred from white superiority.

HOW DOES WHITE APATHY SHOW UP?

Here are a few examples of white apathy in action:

- Using the excuses of laziness, tiredness, fear, boredom, numbness, or perfectionism, turning away from the news, and other apathetic feelings and actions when it comes to engaging in antiracism practice.

- Doing very little antiracism work and therefore not understanding just how urgent this work is.

- Practicing white silence, white exceptionalism, and inaction because of your attachment to the idea that you are a "good white person."

- Using your high sensitivity, high introversion, or mental health and personal issues to opt out of doing the work, ignoring the fact that there are BIPOC who are also highly sensitive, highly introverted, and have mental health and personal issues who cannot opt out of being at the receiving end of (your) racism.

- Not taking personal responsibility for your own antiracism education (i.e., not seeking out books, podcasts, videos, films, articles, classes, and other resources that can support you in growing your understanding about racism and how to dismantle white supremacy).

- Overcomplicating what it takes to practice antiracism, using various excuses that allow you to procrastinate or become over-whelmed by the work that needs to be done.

- Minimizing the effects of racism by telling yourself "it's not that bad" or that BIPOC are "playing the race card."

- Being outspoken on issues not related to racism but silent on issues that affect BIPOC. An example of this in recent history is the groundswell of white women who showed up for the first Women's March protest in the United States on January 21, 2017 (the day after President Donald Trump's inauguration) versus how many of these women show up for protests such as Black Lives Matter.

- Using perfectionism to avoid doing the work and fearing using your voice or showing up for antiracism work until you know everything perfectly and can avoid being called out for making mistakes.

- Feeling frustrated and uncomfortable from realizing that there are no easy or safe solutions in this work. This frustration can lead to a sense of apathy by thinking, "What's the point?"

- Using the excuse that because you did not create white suprem-acy, it is not your job to work on dismantling it.

- Using the excuse that because the process of dismantling white supremacy is so overwhelming, with many parts out of your individual control, there is no point in even trying because it will not make an impact big enough to matter anyway.

WHY DO YOU NEED TO LOOK AT WHITE APATHY?

White apathy is another important component that keeps white supremacy in place as the status quo. White supremacy keeps people with white privilege numb and apathetic to really doing this work. It is not that you did not care about BIPOC. It is that you did not care *enough* for it to be a high priority. There is no personal gain for people with white privilege to do this work and a lot to lose in terms of privilege and power.

Politicians who use the fear of "the other" to stoke up support are tapping into this fear of losing privilege. These politicians drive a rhetoric that says if we let these people in and give them the privileges and power that we have, they will take everything away from us—our jobs, our homes, our wealth, our safety, and everything that makes us who we are. Though this racist rhetoric sounds vile to you on a conscious level and you do not support politicians like that, on an unconscious level, white supremacy is telling you the same thing. And you have bought it, hook, line, and sinker. White supremacy is telling you not to fight for what is right, not to involve yourself with the dismantling of a system that benefits you, because if you do, you will lose everything that makes you who you think you are—a person who has been conditioned to believe you are superior to people of other races. The conditioned mind wants to cling to what it knows and what has kept it safe, even at the risk of harming other people in the process.

To fight against your white apathy is to fight against white supremacy. To resist the urge to make excuses, stay detached, retreat into silence, avoid responsibility, and accept the complexities of this work is to show up for the practice of antiracism.

Reflective Journaling Prompts

1. In what ways have you been apathetic when it comes to racism?

2. In what ways have you observed people who hold white privilege in your communities (family, friends, work) being apathetic when it comes to racism?

day 16

YOU AND WHITE CENTERING

"I have had reviews in the past that have accused me of not writing about white people...as though our lives have no meaning and no depth without the white gaze. And I've spent my entire writing life trying to make sure that the white gaze was not the dominant one in any of my books."

—TONI MORRISON

WHAT IS WHITE CENTERING?

The above quote is taken from an interview filmed in the 1990s between television journalist and talk show host Charlie Rose and highly acclaimed bestselling author Toni Morrison. During this part of the interview, Morrison was responding to a question she was frustrated with receiving from journalists again and again—"When are you going to write books that are not about race?" In other words, she was being asked when she was going to write books that were not centrally about Black people, outside the white gaze. The subliminal messaging of the question seemed to be that her choice to not include white people as central characters in her novels and her choice not to tackle Blackness through the lens of whiteness somehow made her work lower class, less mainstream, and less relevant. Because her writing did not center whiteness as the hero of the story or the primary question that Black people should be concerned with, it was being judged as being somehow less believable. In the interview, Morrison goes on to explain that white writers like Leo Tolstoy also wrote about race but that because "white is not seen as a race, nobody ever questions when white writers will write outside of whiteness."[36]

I remember watching this interview a few years ago and being profoundly struck by Morrison's answers. It made me realize how white is seen as "normal" and nonwhite is seen as "other." I was frustrated that the underlying question to Morrison seemed to be "When are you going to put aside your Blackness and write about things that are more relevant to white people?" And it made me think about all the other ways I witnessed white centering as a normal part of life. Think about the movies, books, podcasts, television shows, magazines, wellness spaces, and leaders you come across every day. Who is overrepresented? Who is underrepresented? Who is seen as the norm, and who is seen as marginal?

When I began interviewing mainly Black women and Women of Color on my podcast, I sometimes received the question from people with white privilege—is this podcast for us? It made me wonder, when a podcast features mainly white interview guests, am I supposed to question whether the podcast is for me? This is an example of white centering—the idea that when a creation features mainly white people, it is for everyone, but if it features mainly BIPOC, it is only relevant to BIPOC.

White centering is the centering of white people, white values, white norms, and white feelings over everything and everyone else. If we think back to the definition of white supremacy, white centering makes sense. White supremacy is the idea that people who are white or white-passing are superior to and therefore deserve to dominate over people who are not white. Under white supremacy, whiteness is centered as the norm. Everyone else is seen as marginal. Whiteness is seen as the highest value measure of rightness, goodness, truth, excellence, and worthiness.

White centering is a natural consequence of white supremacy. If you unconsciously believe you are superior, then you will unconsciously believe that your worldview is the one that is superior, normal, right, and that it deserves to be at the center.

Self-centering is a natural thing that we all do as individual human beings. Our egos make us see things from a self-centered view: How is this important to *me* as an individual? However, white centering is a collective ego that asks the question how is this important to *us* white people? White centering dismisses all other narratives as less important, which was exactly what Morrison was consciously choosing to subvert when she said, "I've spent my entire writing life trying to make sure that the white gaze was not the dominant one in any of my books."[37] This is not something that people with white privilege have to consciously think about or intentionally choose. Under white supremacy, nonwhite narratives are usually seen as less relevant, except for when being co-opted through cultural appropriation or being reimagined through a white lens.

HOW DOES WHITE CENTERING SHOW UP?

Here are a few examples of white centering in action:

- The overrepresentation of people with white privilege and white-centered narratives in movies, art, books, and other creative arenas.

- The overrepresentation of people with white privilege in positions of leadership and success.

- White feminism (to be covered on Day 22), a type of feminism that centers on the struggle of gender only, because race is not a source of oppression or discrimination for people with white privilege.

- The reinterpretation of historical events and culturally significant holidays through a white-centered narrative that erases or minimizes the narratives of BIPOC, like the American holiday of Thanksgiving, the Australian holiday of Australia Day, or the Dutch holiday of St. Nicholas's Eve.

- White saviorism (to be covered later in this book), which reframes BIPOC as less civilized and less advanced than white people and therefore needing to be "saved" by white people who are seen as more civilized and more advanced.

- Tone policing, as it asks BIPOC to speak in tones that are considered acceptable to those with white privilege.

- The affirmation and valuing of European standards of beauty over BIPOC standards (e.g., straight hair, blue eyes, white or light skin, smaller nose).

- In antiracism work, the focus on how antiracism work makes people with white privilege feel over how racism makes BIPOC feel. White apathy is a form of white centering, as it is more focused on how tiring and overwhelming antiracism is for people with white privilege over how harmful and abusive racism is to BIPOC.

- The response of #AllLivesMatter or #BlueLivesMatter to #BlackLivesMatter, not understanding that the social justice movement would not have to exist if all lives were treated as if they mattered equally.

- The reaction of white fragility when BIPOC-only spaces are created, when white feelings are ignored during racial conversations, when hashtags like #BlackGirlMagic are used, when cultural appropriation is called out, when BIPOC are in leadership positions.

WHY DO YOU NEED TO LOOK AT WHITE CENTERING?

Like a fish cannot see the water it is swimming in and like we human beings cannot see the air we breathe, white centering is like an invisible net holding up white supremacy. While it is easy to see and point out the active racist who uses racial slurs, it is almost impossible to see the everyday racism that marginalizes and erases BIPOC through white centering. White centering is so normal that it barely registers as something that needs to be interrupted or disrupted, and that is exactly what makes it such a dangerous part of white supremacy.

White centering is only invisible to those who have not been taught to see it. The question is, when you see it, will you choose to intentionally disrupt it, or will you turn toward the warm comfort of white apathy? Disrupting white centering begins with disrupting how white centering happens in your own mind and in your own behaviors. As you consider today's topic, ask yourself: Do you give more credence, respect, worth, and energy to people with white privilege and white-centered narratives over BIPOC and BIPOC-centered narratives? Do you question, dismiss, or feel ambivalence toward BIPOC when they interrupt your white-centered world view? Do you make an intentional effort to interrupt white centering when you see it, such as by demanding more representation of BIPOC? During your antiracism work, do you focus more on how you feel over what racism feels like for BIPOC? When you learn what white centering is, you can learn how to decenter whiteness and thereby interrupt white supremacy.

White supremacy makes people with white privilege fear their whiteness being decentered because they have been taught to believe that if they are not centered, then they are being marginalized and oppressed. But decentering whiteness does not mean becoming inferior to BIPOC. This idea simply feeds into the hierarchical paradigm that drives white supremacy—that one race must be above the others. Decentering whiteness means learning to stop upholding whiteness as the norm and instead learning to live and operate in a more inclusive way.

White supremacy does not want equality; it wants dominance. And that is why it is so hard and so important to decenter whiteness. Because in the decentering, BIPOC are given space to be treated as equals. When whiteness is decentered, white supremacy loses its power.

Reflective Journaling Prompts

1. How is your worldview a white-centered one?

2. How have you reacted when whiteness or you as a white person are not centered in spaces and conversations?

3. How have you judged BIPOC when they do not measure up to white-centered standards?

4. How have you centered yourself as a person with white privilege in nonwhite spaces and conversations?

5. What are you beginning to understand about how white centering affects BIPOC?

---

day 17

YOU AND TOKENISM

"The norm is white, apparently, in the view
of people who see things in that way. For
them, the only reason you would introduce
a black character is to introduce this kind
of abnormality. Usually, it's because you're
telling a story about racism or at least race."

—OCTAVIA BUTLER

WHAT IS TOKENISM?

My children, who were both born in and have grown up in Qatar,
attend the same British curriculum school that I graduated from.
Despite being a British school, the student body is extremely
diverse. During my years as a student, I can recall more than fifty
different nationalities being represented. When we first moved to

Qatar from the U.K., I was in awe at meeting children who were from all over the world. I was no longer the "only." My cultural difference was just like every other student's. It has been almost two decades since I graduated, and the student body seems to be even more diverse than it was when I was a student. And I am grateful that my children have had the experience from day one of their education journey of not being the only children of color in their class or school.

However, while the student body is wonderfully diverse, the teaching and leadership body is not. I cannot recall having had a single teacher who was a Person of Color during my time as a student, and while there are more teachers of color now, they are still the minority. At a recent parents' assembly where the school's board presented the updates for the academic year, I decided to raise this as an issue. I asked why it was that the teaching body was so white and what was being done to bring in more teachers of color. I shared that it was important for my children, and in fact *all* children, to have more teachers of color. Separately, months earlier, I had raised an issue at another parents' assembly because I was unhappy that the reading curriculum for my daughter's year group featured novels from authors and fictional characters who were mainly white. In both cases, I received a sympathetic yet lukewarm response that they understood it was an issue and they would see what they could do about it. They also shared that there had been efforts to bring in more teachers of color. But as a parent of the school, all I had ever seen were a few token teachers of color. Enough that they could say they were trying but not enough to come anywhere near to real diversity and inclusion.

I was left with the impression that while they could understand it was a problem, it was not a big enough problem for them. I felt as though the most that would be done would be to add a few more token teachers of color and books by authors of color to satisfy the "look" of diversity without doing the deeper work needed for true inclusivity and representation.

Why is it important to me that my children have an inclusive mix of teachers to learn from through the academic years? Shouldn't I be satisfied that the student body is diverse? While I am happy that the student body is so diverse, I also understand that children are influenced by who they see in positions of leadership and authority as well as who they see in fictional stories. I am also aware that unconscious racial bias and anti-Blackness from teachers with white privilege does not magically disappear because they have such a diverse student body. The school's response to my requests did not surprise me. Calls for greater inclusivity and representation from BIPOC are usually met with similar responses, regardless of whether at a school, in a company, or even at an awards ceremony (#OscarsSoWhite).

Tokenism is defined as "the practice of making only a perfunctory or symbolic effort to do a particular thing, especially by recruiting a small number of people from underrepresented groups in order to give the appearance of sexual or racial equality within a workforce."[38] In the case of white supremacy, tokenism essentially uses BIPOC as props or meaningless symbols to make it look like antiracism is being practiced while continuing to maintain the status quo of white as the dominant norm. As calls for diversity grow across different industries, media, and communities, tokenism becomes more rampant. In an effort to fix the problem of underrepresentation, organizations use tokenism as a handy Band-Aid to fix a problem that has much deeper roots.

Tokenism is not just a tactic used by organizations and brands. It is also something that individuals with white privilege use to prove their white exceptionalism and status as a nonracist person. People may use their BIPOC family member, friend, teacher, person they voted for, or even antiracist author or educator they follow to prove they are not racist. But proximity to and even intimacy with BIPOC does not erase white privilege, unconscious bias, or complicity in the system of white supremacy. Being in a relationship with a BIPOC or having a biracial or multiracial child does not absolve a person with white privilege from the practice of antiracism.

HOW DOES TOKENISM SHOW UP?

There are four types of tokenism that we often see:

Brand Tokenism

When a predominantly white organization or event engages a few token BIPOC or uses BIPOC cultural elements to give the visual effect of diversity without being actually committed to inclusion or antiracism in practice or policy. What we often see are swift moves to bring in BIPOC for the front end of the business, brand, or event without committing to longer-term antiracism practice or policy change. BIPOC are used for photo opportunities and the number count but not engaged with in a meaningful way beyond their usability as tokens.

Storytelling Tokenism

When BIPOC characters are used on-screen to give the visual look of diversity or to supplement the main white characters. This type of tokenism is often seen in movies, on television, and even in books, as Octavia Butler pointed out in today's opening quote. These characters' roles and story lines are often underdeveloped or lacking in depth or nuance, as pointed out by Viola Davis when we covered anti-Blackness against Black women on Day 9.

Emotional Labor Tokenism

When a person or group of people with white privilege or a predominantly white organization places the burden on token BIPOC to carry the emotional labor of discussing and working on all matters related to racism, thus reducing them simply to their race. This does not refer to a BIPOC whose paid work is intentionally focused on race but rather someone who happens to be BIPOC and is therefore expected to answer all questions related to their experiences of racism.

Relational Tokenism

When a person with white privilege uses their proximity to and relationships with BIPOC as proof that they are not racist: "I can't be racist because my partner/ex/children/family members/best friends/teachers/favorite writers, entertainers, activists, athletes, entrepreneurs, etc. are BIPOC."

WHY DO YOU NEED TO LOOK AT TOKENISM?

In all cases of tokenism, BIPOC are used as token props to prove one's nonracism. It goes without saying that this is dehumanizing because it strips away BIPOC's humanity and treats them as "get out of racism free cards" that can be whipped out at any time. It is particularly insidious when used against another BIPOC, because it weaponizes one BIPOC against another (e.g., a Black woman calls you out on your racism, and you respond with the fact that you have a Black child/best friend/partner, so you cannot be racist).

Tokenism of BIPOC is a white supremacist act because it still places BIPOC as objects that can be used to further a white person's or organization's agenda, and it protects people with white privilege from having to do the work of disrupting white dominance. Tokenism looks flattering on the outside, but the truth of it is that it uses BIPOC as if they are things, not people. Tokenism says that BIPOC are only valuable to people with white privilege to the degree that they can be used for their own agenda (whether consciously or unconsciously).

Greater inclusivity and representation in all spaces is something that we all want to strive for. However, when it comes without a real commitment to practicing antiracism on a deeper level, what inevitably happens is that BIPOC who have been tokenized are harmed in the process. The experience of being tokenized by people with white privilege is very painful for BIPOC. It causes BIPOC to ask "Have I been invited to participate here because of what I have to contribute through the value I can add or because I will help to tick off a diversity checkbox?"

Without understanding what tokenism is and committing not to practice it, white supremacy continues to control the narrative about what equality and dignity for BIPOC look like.

Reflective Journaling Prompts

1. How have you justified your racism by using your proximity to BIPOC?

2. How have you tokenized BIPOC to prove your words, thoughts, or actions are not racist?

3. How have you tokenized and weaponized one BIPOC against another BIPOC?

4. If you are a business owner, how have you tokenized BIPOC or BIPOC culture in your brand?

5. If you believe you have never tokenized BIPOC, how have you stayed silent when you saw it happening?

6. When you have lauded organizations or events for being diverse because they appear to have a few BIPOC, how much further have you looked into their actual practices and policies toward BIPOC? How have you mistaken the look of diversity for actual inclusivity and equity?

day 18

YOU AND WHITE SAVIORISM

"Funny. Slave masters thought they were making
a difference in black people's lives too. Saving
them from their 'wild African ways.' Same shit,
different century. I wish people like them would
stop thinking that people like me need saving."

—ANGIE THOMAS, *THE HATE U GIVE*

WHAT IS WHITE SAVIORISM?

At the beginning of 2018, during a briefing meeting with lawmakers
in the Oval Office discussing the protection of immigrants from
Haiti, El Salvador, and African countries, U.S. president Donald
Trump asked, "Why do we want all these people from shithole
countries coming here?"[39]

The question shocked people around the world, but in truth,

his comment was reflective of what is often thought but not overtly said about BIPOC. This idea that BIPOC countries and people are inferior in worth, capability, intelligence, and self-determination as compared to white-dominated countries and people with white privilege is a foundational aspect of white supremacy. This sentiment is what leads to *white saviorism*—the belief that people with white privilege, who see themselves as superior in capability and intelligence, have an obligation to "save" BIPOC from their supposed inferiority and helplessness.

The clearest illustration of this concept is what writer Teju Cole has called the "White Savior Industrial Complex."[40] This term describes the phenomenon of well-intentioned white missionaries and volunteers (through the business of voluntourism) traveling to countries in Africa, Asia, and Latin America to help "rescue" BIPOC from their country's poverty and lack of development. Though well-meaning, such volunteers often travel to these countries with not much more than their passion and their desire to do good. Little regard is paid to understanding the historical background and cultural contexts they are entering. Much emphasis is placed on such volunteers having the right solutions to the country's issues without listening to and partnering with the people they intend to help.

Further, a lot of importance is placed on white centering. People with white privilege believe that just through their presence and their privilege, they have what it takes to rescue BIPOC from the very nuanced and complex issues they are faced with. A story is painted of these countries and their citizens as being poor, underdeveloped, and corrupt. Nothing is showcased of their development and technological advancements, nor their thinkers, activists, business leaders, creatives, scientists, or engineers. And most notably, little attention is placed on the impact white supremacist colonialism and imperialism have had on these countries and the issues they are currently facing. Instead, these countries are used as a way for people with white privilege to center themselves as the benevolent saviors, heroes, or messiahs of a people who are destined to live as inferiors unless they are rescued by white intervention. And all it takes is a selfie or two with a Black or Brown child (often without parental consent, or consent without an understanding of how those photos are going to be used to paint a picture of white saviorism) to create this narrative. In his article "The White-Savior Industrial Complex" in *The Atlantic*, Teju Cole explains:

> *One song we hear too often is the one in which Africa serves as a backdrop for white fantasies of conquest and heroism. From the colonial project to Out of Africa to The Constant Gardener and Kony 2012, Africa has provided a space onto which white egos can conveniently be projected. It is a liberated space in which the usual rules do not apply: a nobody from America or Europe can go to Africa and become a godlike savior or, at the very least, have his or her emotional needs satisfied.*[41]

White saviorism is also seen in movies and fictional stories. Movies like *The Last Samurai*, *The Blind Side*, *Avatar*, and *The Help*, among others, center a narrative of a white savior coming to the rescue of BIPOC. Often, these white actors are given characters of great emotional depth and nuance while the BIPOC characters are romanticized with racial tropes or oversimplified cultural contexts. The movie *The Great Wall*, in which actor Matt Damon is the central savior figure in a fictional Chinese story, is another prime example of this. In response to this movie, Asian American actress Constance Wu said, "We have to stop perpetuating the racist myth that only a white man can save the world. It's not based in actual fact. Our heroes don't look like Matt Damon."[42]

White saviorism is not just confined to voluntourism and entertainment, however. The narrative that BIPOC are inferior and helpless without white intervention is present in white supremacist consciousness whether a person with white privilege flies to Africa or stays in their home country. White saviorism at home can show up as teachers with white privilege wanting to rescue their students who are children of color. It can show up as individuals and businesses hosting fund-raisers and nonprofit projects to rescue BIPOC struggling against issues of lack of access and discrimination. And it can even show up as parents with white privilege wanting to adopt children of color (though this is obviously not always the case, it is something to be aware of). In more subtle ways, white saviorism is the person with white privilege speaking over or for BIPOC in the belief that they know better how to say what needs to be said.

HOW DOES WHITE SAVIORISM SHOW UP?

Here are a few examples of white saviorism in action:

- Missionary and voluntourism trips to BIPOC countries with the intention to do good but little preparation on how to serve instead of lead.

- White savior hero narratives in movies, television, and fictional stories.

- Feeling the urge to step in and speak on behalf of BIPOC's needs rather than leaving them with the agency to speak for themselves.

- The belief and perpetuation of a narrative (whether conscious or unconscious) that BIPOC are from "shithole countries" full of poverty, underdevelopment, and corruption.

- The centering of white narratives on BIPOC liberation, such as the belief that nonwhite Muslim women who freely choose to wear the hijab need to be freed from their so-called oppression by ditching the hijab and embracing Western white feminism.

- People with white privilege treating BIPOC and the issues of discrimination they are facing as pet projects to assuage white guilt and center themselves as the hero. For example, upon becoming aware of the Black maternal health crisis in the United States, a white woman told a Black woman I know that she wanted to set up a nonprofit to tackle the crisis. This desire, though seemingly well-meaning, completely disregards the fact that there are already Black women and people leading this work and that as a person with white privilege, a better way for her to support the healing of this crisis would be to do her own antiracism work and approach these organizations to ask them how she can best support them. The desire to become the hero of the story is a common one.

WHY DO YOU NEED TO LOOK AT WHITE SAVIORISM?

White saviorism seems benign on the surface: Trying to help the marginalized. Trying to "give a voice to the voiceless." Trying to advocate for people who "cannot advocate for themselves." In reality, though, white saviorism is another form of white supremacy.

White saviorism puts BIPOC in the patronizing position of helpless children who need people with white privilege to save them. It implies that without white intervention, instruction, and guidance, BIPOC will be left helpless. That without whiteness, BIPOC, who are seen as inferior to people with white privilege in the white imagination, will not survive.

White saviorism is condescending and an attempt to assuage one's own white guilt. It may look like an attempt to make things right, but it only serves to empower people with white privilege by making them feel better about themselves. It is actively disempowering to BIPOC and continues to reinforce the white supremacist ideas that BIPOC are only useful to the extent that they can be used for white interest (tokenism) and that white people are more capable of knowing what is best for BIPOC than they know for themselves (white superiority).

White saviorism is a form of colonialism. It is also a narrative contortion—people with white privilege have historically colonized, harmed, abused, kidnapped, enslaved, and marginalized BIPOC. White saviorism sweeps this under the rug and then rewrites the script.

Reflective Journaling Prompts

1. What white savior narratives have you noticed yourself buying into (whether consciously or unconsciously)?

2. In what ways have you believed that BIPOC are helpless and require intervention and help from people with white privilege?

3. In what ways have you tried to intervene or offer instruction or guidance, believing that your (superior white) view would offer the best solutions?

4. In what ways have you spoken over BIPOC or for them because you felt that you could explain their needs and experiences better than they could? In what ways have you put BIPOC words through a white filter?

5. How have you unconsciously thought about dismantling racism as something that you needed to give your "help" to as a good white savior?

6. What has your reaction been when BIPOC have told you or other people with white privilege that they do not need your "help" and that instead they need you to listen, do the work, and follow BIPOC leadership? What reactions have you noticed coming up (e.g., white fragility, tone policing, white exceptionalism, white superiority, etc.)?

day 19

YOU AND OPTICAL ALLYSHIP

"Racism should never have happened and so
you don't get a cookie for reducing it."

—CHIMAMANDA NGOZI ADICHIE, *AMERICANAH*

WHAT IS OPTICAL ALLYSHIP?

While facilitating the live #MeAndWhiteSupremacy Instagram
challenge, I received a message from a white woman inviting me
to speak at a spiritual women's festival in the U.K. She began her
message by praising me and the work that I was doing through the
challenge and then went on to explain that they were interested in
bringing me in to speak because they had come to realize that they
needed more diverse voices. A quick Google search of the festival
showed me that the organizers, hosts, and speakers of the conference were mainly people with white privilege. I was wary about

entering such a space that had historically lacked BIPOC representation and, more notably, that had not to date had meaningful and challenging conversations about race. I was also curious as to whether she had been engaging in the challenge, because despite her compliments, I had not seen her name before.

In response to the invitation, my team and I asked two questions. First, was she doing the #MeAndWhiteSupremacy challenge? Her answer to this question would help me to know if she understood the nature of this work and how disruptive it can be for a predominantly white space like the one she was inviting me into. And second, I wanted to know whether the festival had any policies or practices in place that would protect me as a Black woman entering into this largely white space to talk about race. I wanted to know if they would make efforts to ensure that I was not on the receiving end of racial microaggressions like the ones we have talked about so far in this book.

In her response to us, the woman answered first that she was not participating in the challenge. However, she wanted me to know that she was an ally who had been involved in this work for a very long time. This was my first warning sign. In response to the second question, she told us that no, they did not have such policies in place, because they "can't protect from people being assholes." This was my second warning sign that she did not understand what white supremacy is or what practicing allyship looks like. She wanted to bring me in as a token to add a "diverse voice" so the festival would look as though it was practicing antiracist allyship, but she did not want to do the deeper work—both personally and organizationally—to ensure that this act of allyship did not end up in me being on the receiving end of white fragility and other racial microaggressions. She used compliments, flattery, and a declaration that she was an ally to invite me in, but when asked how I would be protected coming into a space like that, she had nothing. This is an example of optical allyship.

Maybe you have heard of the terms *performative allyship* or *ally theater* before. Optical allyship is another term for this behavior and can be used interchangeably with those terms. My friend Latham Thomas, author and founder of Mama Glow, a premier maternity lifestyle brand, introduced me to the term *optical allyship* in May 2018, and it has stuck with me ever since. In a social media post she shared at that time called "We are not interested in Optical Allyship," Thomas defined *optical allyship* as "allyship that only serves at the surface level to platform the 'ally,' it makes a statement but doesn't go beneath the surface and is not aimed at breaking away from the systems of power that oppress." Thomas was speaking to what she saw as the co-opting of social justice movements in an era when being "woke" is now seen as cool. And what she took issue with is people with privilege not doing the deeper work of antioppression but rather using behaviors such as tokenism, white saviorism, white centering, and so on to create an optical illusion of allyship.

There are certain signs that tell us whether an act of allyship is genuine or optical:

- The intention behind the act of allyship is to avoid being called racist and/or to receive a reward through social recognition, praise, and acknowledgment.

- The act of allyship creates the look of diversity and inclusion but does not come with any change at a deeper level through policy change, commitment to antiracism education, transfer of benefits or privilege, etc. The act of allyship is symbolic but not substantive.

- The act of allyship is one that is led by a person with white privilege who is not listening to, partnering with, or following the leadership of the BIPOC they want to help. We see this with white saviorism and the person with white privilege performing an act of allyship that is ultimately about positioning themselves as the benevolent and conscientious hero.

- The act of allyship involves no real risk. It is one that is performed from the safety of one's comfort zone of privilege.

- The person engages in white fragility when challenged by BIPOC to not perform optical allyship rather than listening and taking guidance.

HOW DOES OPTICAL ALLYSHIP SHOW UP?

Here is a nonexhaustive list of examples of optical allyship:

- Jumping into activism without doing any real self-reflection work on your personal racism.

- Creating the look of being an ally by tokenizing BIPOC.

- Reposting antiracism posts and virtue signaling so that everyone knows you're an ally but not doing much more work beyond that.

- Positioning yourself as an ally or activist leader while continuing to step over, talk over, speak for, and take over the spaces of BIPOC.

- Distancing yourself from your own white supremacy by continuously complaining about how awful other white people are.

- Creating campaigns and movements for antiracism that are really about building your social capital or assuaging your white guilt.

- Only showing up for the fun, easy, glamorous work and disappearing when it's time to do the real work.

- Clinging to symbols like pink pussy hats, safety pins, and hashtags over doing the real work.

- Bringing activism words and BIPOC images into your brand to make your business look more "woke."

- Reading this book today because you secretly hope it will make you look more "woke."

- Acting like an ally in public but harming BIPOC behind closed doors.

- Going out of your way to be *extra* nice to BIPOC with the hopes you will be seen as a "good white person."

- Only sharing the work of BIPOC who you've deemed to be palatable to the white gaze.

WHY DO YOU NEED TO LOOK AT OPTICAL ALLYSHIP?

Like with tokenism and white saviorism, optical allyship is all about the person with white privilege and not the BIPOC it is intended to support. It is about how it makes you look and feel. It is not a form of antiracist practice, despite how it looks. It is another form of white centering. It is a way to continue to affirm yourself as a person of white privilege while either not actually being an ally to BIPOC or actively doing harm to BIPOC.

Tokenism, white saviorism, and optical allyship all seem on the surface like really great ways to combat racism. However, underneath the surface, they continue to perpetuate the ideologies that white supremacy rests on—that in the end, any actions taken must somehow benefit those with white privilege at the expense of, to the detriment of, and on the backs of BIPOC.

The website Guide to Allyship gives a clear and simple explanation about what allyship actually looks like. Created and curated by product designer and writer Amélie Lamont, the site defines *allyship* as:

* Taking on the struggle as your own

* Standing up, even when you feel scared

* Transferring the benefits of your privilege to those who lack it

* Acknowledging that while you, too, feel pain, the conversation is not about you

While optical allyship centers people with privilege, actual allyship centers those who are marginalized.

Reflective Journaling Prompts

1. How have you practiced optical allyship when it comes to antiracism?

2. What benefits have you sought out and/or received by practicing optical allyship?

3. How have you responded when called out for optical allyship?

4. How have you felt when you have not been rewarded for your acts of optical allyship?

5. How has your motivation to show up in allyship been dependent upon what other people think about you or how you are perceived?

day 20

YOU AND BEING
CALLED OUT/CALLED IN

> "Mistakes are a fact of life. It is the
> response to error that counts."
>
> —NIKKI.GIOVANNI

WHAT IS BEING CALLED OUT OR CALLED IN?

On Day 2 we talked about white fragility, which Robin DiAngelo defined as "a state in which even a minimum amount of racial stress becomes intolerable, triggering a range of defensive moves."[43] White fragility is frequently experienced when being called out or called in.

Call outs and calls in are both methods of calling attention to problematic, harmful, and oppressive behaviors with the ultimate aim being changed behavior and the making of amends. Writer, poet, and community organizer Asam Ahmad, in his 2015 article in *Briarpatch* magazine called "A Note on Call-Out Culture," defines the two terms as follows: "Call-out culture refers to the tendency among progressives, radicals, activists, and community organizers to publicly name instances or patterns of oppressive behavior and language use by others...calling in means speaking privately with an individual who has done some wrong, in order to address the behavior without making a spectacle of the address itself."[44]

Much has been written about the merits and critiques of calling out versus calling in, with debates on which method is most effective. These arguments are nuanced and complicated and include factors such as:

- Power dynamics

- Tone policing

- Respectability often expected from BIPOC

- The nature of the relationship that exists between the person being called out/in and the person calling out/in

- The level of emotional labor involved for BIPOC

- The toxicity that can come with call-out culture versus call outs sometimes being the best and only approach available.

- Optical allyship being employed

That all being said, what we are going to focus on today is not whether it is better to call out or to call in, but rather your reaction to being called out or called in.

None of us are born fully conscious of systems of oppression or our own privileges and unconscious biases. We are also not born aware of the historical contexts within which we hold identities of privilege or marginalization. But because there is such a focus on being perfect and doing antiracism perfectly and on being seen as good person, people with white privilege often cause more harm when being called out/in because their white fragility causes them not to receive the feedback necessary to listen, apologize, and do better going forward.

It is normal for any person who has been informed (whether through being called out or called in) that they have caused harm to become defensive, especially when causing harm was not intended. We all react the same way: sweaty palms, accelerated heart rate, the "warm wash of shame" coming over us (as research professor and author Brené Brown calls it), feeling nauseous, and an immediate reaction to want to stand up and defend ourselves by explaining our intentions. Believing we are under attack, our brains react quickly with a fight-or-flight response, causing a cascade of stress hormones to be released into our bodies. However, these feelings are more exacerbated during racial conversations because of the existence of white fragility, white superiority, white exceptionalism, and so on. While call outs and calls in never feel good, they are an invitation to become aware of behaviors and beliefs that are hidden to you, and they are an opportunity to do better so that you can stop doing harm and make amends for the pain caused.

We have all had the experience of stepping on someone's foot or bumping into someone and immediately apologizing. It was not our *intention* to hurt them, but it is understood that the *impact* is still that harm was caused. Instead of refusing to apologize because we did not mean it, we rush to apologize because we understand we have caused pain. This is a very oversimplified explanation of what happens when we cause people harm. However, I find it useful as an easy way of understanding how, when we have caused harm, our impact matters more than our intention. So when we talk about being called out or called in, a common reaction by people with white privilege is to focus on their intention rather than their impact on BIPOC. This is a form of white centering, which prioritizes how a person of privilege feels about being called out/in versus the actual pain that BIPOC experience as a result of that person's actions, whether intentional or unintentional.

HOW DO REACTIONS TO BEING CALLED OUT AND CALLED IN SHOW UP?

Here are a few examples of reactions to being called out or called in:

- Becoming defensive, derailing, crying, falling silent, or dramatically leaving the space or conversation.

- Focusing on intent while ignoring or minimizing impact.

- Tone policing BIPOC by claiming you are being attacked or characterizing the person(s) calling you out as aggressive and irrational.

- Denying that your actions were racist because you "do not see color" (color blindness).

- Tokenizing BIPOC to prove you are not racist or talking about all the good things you have done for BIPOC (proving that these acts were actually optical allyship).

- Talking more than listening to the people calling you out/in.

- Focusing on how you can quickly fix things through optical ally-ship rather than really taking the time to reflect on your actions and do further research on what you are being called out/in for.

WHY DO YOU NEED TO LOOK AT BEING CALLED OUT AND CALLED IN?

White supremacy (especially white superiority, white centering, and white exceptionalism) positions people with white privilege as virtuous, nice, and morally right. To be called out or called in feels like a dangerous attack against the individual and the collective identity of whiteness. It threatens you as a person with white privilege and the concept of white supremacy as a whole. And when the call out/call in comes from BIPOC, toward whom you unconsciously hold feelings of anti-Blackness and racial inferiority, it is easy to dismiss, hold suspicion against, or simply not believe them.

If you do not examine your own reactions to being called out/in, then you will stay in a state of fragility, and you will continue to weaponize this fragility against BIPOC by centering yourself as the victim and refusing to apologize or change your behavior. This keeps white supremacy firmly in place.

By continuing to focus on your intent and your feelings, you practice the belief that you matter more than BIPOC. That your feelings of discomfort about being called out/in matter more than the pain that BIPOC experience at the hands of racism.

The fear of being called out/in is a dangerous deterrent to genuine antiracism practice. If you are constantly afraid of doing the wrong thing and being called out/in for it, then your antiracism work will easily slip into perfectionism, which will lead to:

• **White fragility**, because you have not built the resilience needed for doing this work.

• **Tone policing**, because you can only handle being called out/in if the message is delivered to you in a certain tone.

• **White silence**, because of the fear of saying the wrong thing.

• **White exceptionalism**, because you will continue to think you are the exception to the rule, "one of the good ones."

• **White apathy**, because you will think "What is the point if I am going to be called out/in?"

• **Tokenism**, because you will want a BIPOC to protect you from the pain of being called out/in.

• **Optical allyship**, because you will be more concerned with not being called out/in than with simply doing the work.

You *will* be called out/in as you do antiracism work. Making mistakes is how you learn and do better going forward. Being called out/in is not a deterrent to the work. It is part of the work. And there is no safety in this work. There has been no safety for BIPOC under white supremacy. And the sense of perceived emotional danger that people with white privilege feel when being called out/in is so small compared to what BIPOC experience through racism.

The questions today are these: When (not if) you are called out/in, are you well-equipped enough to respond to it in a way that will help you learn and do better, or will you simply give in to white fragility and fall apart? Are you willing to do the work to set aside your unconscious beliefs around your racial superiority and exceptionalism and really listen to BIPOC with empathy and a desire to do better? Will you put in the work to educate yourself so that as you continue to grow and learn, you will do more good than harm?

Reflective Journaling Prompts

1. What have you felt, thought, said, or done when called out/in? How have you centered yourself and your intentions over BIPOC and the impact of your actions?

2. If it has not happened to you yet, how do you think you will react when it happens, based on your level of self-awareness, personal antiracism work, and white fragility?

3. When you have been called out/in, how have you handled apologizing and making amends?

4. What are your biggest fears about being called out/in?

5. Think back over the topics we have covered so far in this book. What behaviors and beliefs most get in your way of being able to respond appropriately to being called out/in?

day 21

WEEK 3 REVIEW

This week, we covered behaviors related to the practice of allyship and how white supremacy can continue to be perpetuated in actions and behaviors that seem noble or neutral in theory but quickly reveal a foundation of the racist status quo being maintained underneath.

White apathy, like white silence, is a passive way of continuing to be complicit in white supremacy through nonaction. White apathy says BIPOC are not important enough for you to show up, use your voice, and do the work. This collective lack of energy toward antiracism and social change is what keeps white supremacy locked in place.

White centering upholds white supremacy by maintaining the dominance of whiteness as the norm and by focusing energy on prioritizing the needs and desires of people with white privilege above everyone else. Tokenism, white saviorism, and optical allyship show us, on the other hand, that it is possible to *intend* to do the right thing while continuing to perpetuate white centering and white superiority. In exploring these topics, you have a greater understanding of how to show up in ways that do more good than harm.

And lastly, because doing this work means you will make mistakes, we looked at how you react when being called out/in and how to use these moments as opportunities to listen, apologize, become more educated about privilege and oppression, and do better going forward. Maya Angelou famously said, "Do the best you can until you know better. Then when you know better, do better."[45] When it comes to racial conversations, that means beginning with the willingness to lay down white fragility and unconscious bias, listen to the feedback being offered (even though it causes discomfort), reflect on your actions and unconscious beliefs, educate yourself, apologize, make amends through changed behavior, and do better in the future.

Reflective Journaling Prompts

1. What more have you learned about yourself and your unique, personal brand of white supremacy?

2. In what ways have you realized behaviors you have thought were "not that bad" were actually very harmful?

3. Where are you beginning to see your biggest challenge is when it comes to your personal antiracism work?

4. Where are you starting to do your work, and where are you still holding back?

5. What other dots have you started connecting when reflecting on the work you have done so far?

week 4

POWER, RELATIONSHIPS, AND COMMITMENTS

In our final week together, we look at your relationships with other people with white privilege as well as your personal values and commitments to antiracism. Some of the days during this week are shorter than the ones we have covered during other weeks. This is because less explanation is needed about the particular topic and more emphasis is placed on reflecting on your relationships with other people and your own commitments going forward.

Over the last three weeks, we have covered a lot of different intersecting behaviors, beliefs, and dynamics that make up white supremacy. As we come into our final week, it is time to bring this learning together in ways that can best support you after completing this book. Take a moment to review what you have covered so far, as it will help you to go deeper in answering some of the reflective questions.

day 22

YOU AND WHITE FEMINISM

"If feminism can understand the patriarchy,
it's important to question why so many
feminists struggle to understand whiteness as
a political structure in the very same way."

—RENI EDDO-LODGE, *WHY I'M NO LONGER
TALKING TO WHITE PEOPLE ABOUT RACE*

WHAT IS WHITE FEMINISM?

As a feminist, I cannot complete this book without talking about feminism. In this context, we are talking about white feminism or what you may have often considered "mainstream" feminism. I understand that each person has their own unique relationship (or absence of relationship) with feminism. Whatever your gender identity or the nature of your relationship with feminism, it is important to explore this topic and its ramifications on BIPOC.

Let us begin with some brief definitions so that we have a common starting ground to build upon. *Feminism* is broadly defined as "a range of *political movements, ideologies,* and *social movements* that share a common goal: to define, establish, and achieve the political, economic, personal, and social *equality of the genders.*"[46] *White feminism* is broadly defined as "an *epithet* used to describe *feminist theories* that focus on the struggles of *white* women without addressing distinct forms of *oppression* faced by *ethnic minority* women and women lacking other *privileges.*" [47]

White feminism focuses on the struggles of white women (usually cisgendered) over BIPOC. It is a feminism that is only concerned with disparities and oppression of gender, and it does not take into account disparities and oppression of other intersections that are just as important, including race, class, age, ability, sexual orientation, gender identity, and so on. White feminists will often ask BIPOC to set aside their race and issues with racism and instead band together in sisterhood under the issue of gender and sexism first.

This request ignores two crucial points:

1. White women do not have to consider the implications of their race, because they have white privilege. Race is not an identity where they experience oppression. Rather, it is an identity where they hold power. To ask BIPOC to set aside their race is to ask BIPOC to act as if they are white.

2. To ask BIPOC to focus on gender before race is to ask them to put their different identities in a hierarchical order. But as a Black woman, I am not Black *then* woman. I am Black *and* woman. My womanness cannot erase my Blackness, and my Blackness cannot erase my womanness. Under white

supremacy and patriarchy, or what feminist author and activist bell hooks calls "imperialist white-supremacist capitalist patriarchy,"[48] Women of Color experience discrimination because of both our race and our gender. The privilege of whiteness means only seeing yourself as a woman (if that is your gender identity), because due to white centering, you are seen as "raceless."

White women hold the expectation that Black, Indigenous, and Women of Color (BIWOC) should stand in solidarity under the shared experience of gender discrimination, but as writer Mikki Kendall's viral hashtag points out, #SolidarityIsForWhiteWomen. And white solidarity in the feminist movement is not a new phenomenon. The Western feminist movement has marginalized BIPOC from its very inception.

In the United States, the very first women's rights conference in Seneca Falls in 1848 failed to address the racism faced by BIWOC. In 1870, in response to the ratification of the Fifteenth Amendment, which secured voting rights for men of all races, Anna Howard Shaw, president of the National Women Suffrage Association, argued, "You have put the ballot in the hands of your black men, thus making them political superiors of white women. Never before in the history of the world have men made former slaves the political masters of their former mistresses!"[49]

In 1913, before the first suffrage parade held in Washington, DC, suffragist Alice Paul wrote in response to the idea that white women and Black women march together, "As far as I can see, we must have a white procession, or a Negro procession, or no procession at all."[50] And though white women received the right to vote in 1920 when the Nineteenth Amendment was ratified, because of racial discrimination, Women of Color in some parts of the United States were subject to many restrictions that made it almost impossible for them to vote until the 1965 Voting Rights Act was passed. The feminist movement has, from its very beginnings, been an extension of white supremacy. It has marginalized BIPOC and expected BIWOC to fit themselves into a so-called universal feminism that is in reality white-centered. It is no wonder that many BIWOC find it hard to see themselves in the feminist movement, opting instead for Black feminism, womanism, or no affiliation with the feminist movement at all.

It is tempting to argue that these events were in the past and have no bearing on the current state of the feminist movement. However, feminism and the divide between white women and BIWOC still exist. Just like white supremacy continues to thrive today despite the granting of civil rights, mainstream feminism continues to exclude and marginalize BIWOC. And despite white women experiencing discrimination and oppression under patriarchy, white women also enact discrimination and oppression against BIWOC under white supremacy. This is a hard pill to swallow for many white women, but as we have explored extensively throughout this book, white women have all the privileges and power that come with their race.

Many white women who consider themselves feminists but who have not engaged with antiracism work with much depth often become defensive at being called white feminists. Actress Emma Watson shared her experience of this in a letter to her book club, Our Shared Shelf, when she announced the first book of 2018— Reni Eddo-Lodge's *Why I'm No Longer Talking to White People about Race*. In the letter, she wrote, "When I heard myself being called a 'white feminist' I didn't understand (I suppose I proved their case in point). What was the need to define me—or anyone else for that matter—as a feminist by race? What did this mean? Was I being called racist? Was the feminist movement more fractured than I had understood? I began... panicking."

She then went on to share how her understanding had evolved: "It would have been more useful to spend the time asking myself questions like: What are the ways I have benefited from being white? In what ways do I support and uphold a system that is structurally racist? How do my race, class, and gender affect my perspective? There seemed to be many types of feminists and feminism. But instead of seeing these differences as divisive, I could have asked whether defining them was actually empowering and bringing about better understanding. But I didn't know to ask these questions."[51]

HOW DOES WHITE FEMINISM SHOW UP?

Here are a few examples of white feminism in action:

- White feminists will talk about the pay gap between men and women without referencing the pay gap between white women and BIWOC.

- White feminists will tell BIWOC that talking about race is "divisive" and that we should focus first on being united under gender.

- White feminist spirituality culturally appropriates and white-washes BIPOC spirituality.

- White feminists showed up for women at the 2017 Women's

March but do not show up in similar numbers for Black women
and people at Black Lives Matter marches.

* White feminism largely ignores or is unaware of the Black maternal health crisis because it does not impact white women.

* White feminism centers white women leaders while undermining and betraying BIWOC leaders.

* White feminism ignores or excludes the groundbreaking works
of Black feminist leaders like Kimberlé Crenshaw, Audre Lorde,
bell hooks, Alice Walker, Angela Davis, or other nonwhite
feminists.

* White feminism does not believe that Muslim feminists who
choose to wear the hijab are real feminists.

WHY DO YOU NEED TO LOOK AT WHITE FEMINISM?

White feminism is an extension of white supremacy. It is only
concerned with white women gaining parity with white men, and
throughout history, it has shown that it will throw under the bus
anyone who is not white to gain that parity.

White feminism asks BIWOC to ignore their race and focus
only on their gender. During a speech at the Women's Convention
in Akron, Ohio, in 1851, Sojourner Truth said, "That man over there
says that women need to be helped into carriages, and lifted over
ditches, and to have the best place everywhere. Nobody ever helps
me into carriages, or over mud-puddles, or gives me any best place!

And ain't I a woman?"[52] Truth was asking if her Blackness made her less of a woman, because she was not treated in the same way that white women were treated. And because of white supremacy, this still rings true today. Under white feminism and white supremacy, the only way for BIWOC to gain parity with white women would be to perform an impossibility—to make ourselves raceless in the white imagination.

The antidote to the poison of white feminism and by extension white supremacy is intersectionality. *Intersectionality* is a term coined by law professor and civil rights advocate Dr. Kimberlé Crenshaw. It is a framework that helps us to explore the dynamic between coexisting identities and connected systems of oppression, particularly as it relates to gender and race and the experiences of Black women. Crenshaw explains, "Intersectionality simply came from the idea that if you're standing in the path of multiple forms of exclusion, you are likely to get hit by both. These women are injured, but when the race ambulance and the gender ambulance arrive at the scene, they see these women of color lying in the intersection and they say, 'Well, we can't figure out if this was just race or just sex discrimination. And unless they can show us which one it was, we can't help them.'"[53] Intersectionality gives us a way of practicing feminism that is antiracist. But intersectionality is not something that can be reached without a constant and unwavering commitment to antiracist practice.

Though the term *intersectional feminism* is now used to talk about how people are impacted by systems of oppression, not just gender discrimination and racial discrimination, it cannot be overstated that without a firm commitment to centering BIPOC, intersectionality is meaningless. As Crenshaw said during a speech at Tulane University in 2017, "[Intersectionality] has been gentrified in the sense that people to whom it [was] initially designed to recognize have been pushed out of the discourse… [Women of color] can't be completely pushed in the margins by an idea that was meant to de-marginalize the margins."[54]

Reflective Journaling Prompts

1. To what extent has your idea of feminism been under the issue of gender only?

2. How has your feminism neglected or minimized the issues of BIPOC?

3. How has your feminism rejected, discounted, or simply ignored BIPOC leaders?

4. How has your feminism been white-centered?

5. If you are someone who has called yourself an intersectional feminist, in what ways have you been centering BIWOC?

day 23

YOU AND WHITE LEADERS

> "If we don't challenge each other to use our
> platforms for better than our niches or what
> our quote-unquote brand is, what are we
> doing as influencers? If we can't activate our
> audiences at the times it's important or needed,
> then what do we have these platforms for?"
>
> —LUVVIE AJAYI

YOU AND WHITE LEADERS

Over the last twenty-two prompts, you have dug deep, exploring white supremacist thoughts, beliefs, behaviors, and motivations within yourself. For the next few days of the work, we are examining how these behaviors play out in relationships between you and other people with white privilege in your life and those who have an impact on your life. Today, we are looking at you and white leaders, specifically people with white privilege in positions of leadership, authority, and power whom you come into contact with.

Examples of leaders include teachers, coaches, mentors, authors, speakers, public figures, management at your work or other institutions, worship leaders, community leaders, project leaders, politicians, and so on. It also includes yourself if you are in a leadership position and your peers who are in leadership positions too.

WHY DO YOU NEED TO LOOK AT YOUR RELATIONSHIP WITH WHITE LEADERS?

People with white privilege who are in positions of leadership have a great deal of responsibility. In addition to the white privilege that they already hold, they also have the ability to have a greater impact on how BIPOC are treated, because their voice carries more weight, and their authority means that they sometimes have the ability to create or influence policies and practices. Also, whether right or wrong, we often look to people in positions of leadership as role models of how to be in the world.

However, we can also ask our leaders to do better. When it becomes clear to leaders that their audience, employees, community members, and voters are insisting on change, then they will have no choice but to do the very work you are doing right now. But if everyone stays quiet, nothing changes. The more you do your own antiracism work, the more you can influence white leaders to do their own work too. And the more that they do their antiracism work, the more they will influence other people with white privilege to do their work too.

Reflective Journaling Prompts

1. Knowing what you now know about white supremacist behaviors across Days 1–22, how do you respond when you witness white leaders behaving in these white supremacist ways:

   - *When white leaders tone police BIPOC?*
   - *When white leaders claim color blindness?*
   - *When white leaders use anti-Black tropes or racist stereotypes?*
   - *When white leaders practice cultural appropriation?*
   - *When white leaders practice optical allyship and white saviorism?*

2. When you have witnessed white leaders practicing these behaviors, how do your own white fragility and white silence get in the way of you asking them to do better?

3. How does your fear of loss of privilege and comfort hold you back from asking white leaders to do better?

4. How aware have you been of whether white leaders you follow are doing deeper antiracism work? How much of a priority has it been for you to push them to go beyond the visual effect of diversity?

5. If you are in a leadership position, how do you plan to respond to your own behaviors going forward? How do you plan to hold yourself accountable to doing better?

day 24

YOU AND YOUR FRIENDS

> "There is no social-change fairy. There is only
> change made by the hands of individuals."
>
> —WINONA LADUKE

YOU AND YOUR FRIENDS

Today, we are continuing to look at the personal connections you have and how you respond when you notice white supremacist behaviors playing out. Often times, there is a reluctance to rock the boat by calling in/out racism when you see it, or it is done in such a gentle and subtle way that it is essentially ineffective.

In today's prompt, we are not just talking about your closest friends, as that can often be the easiest place to speak up. There is already built-up rapport, connection, and implicit understanding that the call in/out is not necessarily received as a personal attack (although it can be!).

Instead, I invite you to cast your view out to *all* your friend-ships and acquaintance circles. Your coworkers. Your peers. Other parents in your community. Other students in your school. Other worshippers in your spiritual community. Other entrepreneurs in your business circles. Other artists in your creative circles. Family friends. Your partner's friends. Friends of friends with whom you have spent time. And so on.

WHY DO YOU NEED TO LOOK AT YOUR RELATIONSHIPS WITH YOUR FRIENDS?

In yesterday's topic, we talked about the influence we can have on our leaders. This influence is even greater with our friends. Because of your proximity to and relationships with these people in your life, you have an even greater possibility of being able to influence whether they engage in conscious antiracism practice. In a similar vein, if you practice white silence and white apathy, you influence them to do the same too.

Reflective Journaling Prompts

1. How have you responded when you have witnessed racist words and actions from these people in your life?

2. How have you stayed silent or made excuses for them in your mind?

3. How have you thought it was not worth the hassle because of the discomfort of rocking the boat? Or how have you seen it as your responsibility to address it with them since you have more influence over them because of your friendship?

4. Are there certain people you feel more comfortable speaking up to than others? Why is that?

5. Are there certain people you continue to stay in friendship with even though they are problematic and refuse to change?

6. How have you risked these relationships by calling in/out racist behavior, even if nobody was going to thank you for it?

7. How do you feel about your friends who are not doing their own personal antiracism work?

8. What efforts have you made to invite your friends into doing antiracism work with you?

9. How have you allowed your friends to influence you *not* to engage in antiracism work?

day 25

YOU AND YOUR FAMILY

"No one is born hating another person because
of the color of his skin, or his background,
or his religion. People must learn to hate,
and if they can learn to hate, they can be
taught to love, for love comes more naturally
to the human heart than its opposite."

—NELSON MANDELA

YOU AND YOUR FAMILY

I will preface today's topic by saying that *everyone* has family stuff.
Everyone has family dynamics that range from hurt feelings to
trauma and lots of family secrets. So bringing race and racism into
these dynamics is a lot more complicated than with your friends or
coworkers.

However, your unique and complex family dynamics do not exempt you from doing this work in your family circles. BIPOC have complicated family dynamics too. And on top of that, they still have to deal with racism and white supremacy.

WHY DO YOU NEED TO LOOK AT YOUR RELATIONSHIP WITH YOUR FAMILY?

As with yesterday's topic, your family is where you hold a great deal of influence. It is also the place where you learned—or did not learn—about white privilege and white supremacy. And if you are a parent, it is a place where you hold great influence over how your children, as people with white privilege, will practice or not practice antiracism. Often, a lot of emphasis is placed on having "the big talk" with your family members about racism at annual events such as Thanksgiving or Christmas. However, this is not a one-time conversation. It is an ongoing one that does not just look at calling out the use of racial slurs or cultural appropriation but that also includes deeper discussions on historical and cultural contexts that center whiteness to explore the subtle yet equally harmful white supremacist behaviors we have talked about in this book, such as color blindness, tone policing, white silence, white exceptionalism, and so on. With your more nuanced understanding of how liberal people with white privilege are also complicit in white supremacy from doing this work, you are in a powerful position to help your family members expand and deepen their own antiracism knowledge and practice too.

Reflective Journaling Prompts

1. How do you feel about speaking up about racism and white supremacist beliefs and actions to your family members?

2. How have you excused or ignored your family members' racist behaviors because addressing them seems too difficult and you want to keep the peace?

3. How have you excused your elders' racism because they are "from another time"?

4. If you are a parent, how do you speak to your children about racism beyond "we don't see color"? How early did you or will you speak to your children about racism and white privilege? How early did your parents or caregivers speak to you about racism and white privilege?

5. What racist beliefs have you internalized from your family?

6. To what extent do you place white comfort over antiracism in your family?

7. What are some ways in which you can begin to have deeper conversations with your family about racism?

8. How do you allow perfectionism to get in the way of having racial conversations with your family?

9. In what ways do you (or can you) organize your family to show up for BIPOC in your communities? Not from a place of white saviorism but rather by volunteering at and donating to anti-racist movements and organizations being led by BIPOC in your communities?

day 26

YOU AND YOUR VALUES

"Never forget that justice is what
love looks like in public."

—CORNEL WEST

YOU AND YOUR VALUES

There are now only three days left of this work. However, as you will
have come to realize by now, this work is lifelong. So in these last
days, we are going to look at some areas to help you prepare for staying committed to the work after these twenty-eight days are over.

Today, we are looking at you and your values. Our values are the
principles and standards that guide how we live our lives and where
we choose to place our energy. Our values are our personal set of
beliefs that determine our actions and what is most important to
us in life. Our values are often a mixture of guiding principles we

have chosen for ourselves and those that we have adopted through conditioning (whether societal or religious).

WHY DO YOU NEED TO LOOK AT YOUR VALUES?

Owning white privilege and being conditioned by the system of white supremacy mean that you have some subconscious values that are white supremacist in nature. These values can actually clash with other consciously chosen values that you have.

For example, being conditioned within white supremacy means that one of the values that you likely have is about white superiority—the idea that as a person with white privilege, you are more worthy and deserve to take up more space and resources than BIPOC. At the same time, however, you may have a chosen value that says that you believe that all people are equal and deserve to be treated equally. These two sets of values are at odds with each other and cause you to act in ways that contradict who you think you are and what you believe you value.

Throughout this book, we have been exploring this idea of what it means to be a "good white person." By now, many of you have realized that clinging to this notion has actually done more harm than good, because it has prevented you from doing the real work. When you are so focused on making sure that other people know that you are not racist, you simply continue to practice racism through behaviors like white exceptionalism, tokenism, optical allyship, and white saviorism.

As you come to the end of this book and look at your values, I invite you to define for yourself what it means to be "good" as a person who holds white privilege. I invite you to release the desire to be *seen* as good by other people and instead explore what it looks like for you to own that you are a person who holds privilege and that you are a person who is committed to practicing antiracism.

Reflective Journaling Prompts

1. To what extent have your values helped your ability to practice antiracism?

2. What contradictory values do you hold that hinder your ability to practice antiracism?

3. What new core values and beliefs do you feel you need to integrate after doing this work in order to better practice lifelong antiracism?

4. How has your desire to be seen as a good person with white privilege prevented you from actually being "good"?

day 27

YOU AND LOSING PRIVILEGE

"Whiteness is an advantage and privilege
because you have made it so, not
because the universe demands it."

—MICHAEL ERIC DYSON, *TEARS WE CANNOT STOP:*
A SERMON TO WHITE AMERICA

YOU AND LOSING PRIVILEGE

We are coming full circle now. When you first started this book, Day 1 was all about you and white privilege. Over the last twenty-six days, you have explored what that privilege means in ways that you have probably never done before. You have been able to see how your privilege has harmed BIPOC.

You will also have begun to realize that in order for change to happen, you must lose some of that privilege. I am not talking about "using your privilege for good" in some sort of white saviorist super ally kind of way. This is not about rescuing or saving BIPOC by becoming a "voice for the voiceless." Rather, I am talking about the privileges, advantages, and comforts you must be willing to let go of so that BIPOC can have more dignity in their lives. White privilege is a bubble that protects you, rewards you with unearned advantages, gives you the belief that you are entitled to be in all spaces all the time, shields you from showing up for BIPOC, and grants you a feeling of authority and power.

WHY DO YOU NEED TO LOOK AT LOSING PRIVILEGE?

While the work we have been doing here is important in helping you to deepen your understanding and knowledge about privilege and racism, without actually relinquishing some of that privilege, nothing changes.

Being willing to lose privilege looks like:

- Taking responsibility for your own antiracist education with the free and paid resources already publicly available, instead of expecting BIPOC to do that work for you.

- Talking to your friends and family members who have white privilege about practicing antiracism.

- Having racial conversations with other white people, whether in person or online.

- Donating money to causes, movements, and organizations that are working toward liberation and dignity for BIPOC.

- Paying money to more BIPOC businesses, entrepreneurial ventures, and projects.

- Amplifying BIPOC voices (whether or not their work is about racism and social justice).

- Showing up at protests and marches for BIPOC.

- Calling out/in leaders, organizations, and institutions that are discriminating against and doing harm to BIPOC.

- Continuing to show up, even when you are called out, you feel discomfort or fatigue, or you are not rewarded for it (socially or financially).

- Taking up less space and allowing BIPOC to take up more space so that they can be heard and their leadership can be followed.

- Risking relationships and comfort by speaking up instead of staying silent.

Reflective Journaling Prompts

1. In what ways will your privilege need to change in order for you to consistently practice antiracism?

2. How will you need to change the way you take up space for and with BIPOC?

3. How will you need to show up differently for BIPOC?

4. What risks must you be willing to take? What sacrifices must you be willing to make?

5. What comforts must you be willing to lose?

6. In what ways will you need to take greater responsibility?

7. How will you need to decenter whiteness and the white gaze?

8. How will you need to lose privilege and safety in your friendships, workspaces, businesses, families, spiritual communities, and other white-centered spaces?

9. Are you willing to lose your white privilege after everything you've learned here?

day 28

YOU AND YOUR COMMITMENTS

"The relevant question is not whether all Whites are racist but how we can move more White people from a position of active or passive racism to one of active antiracism."

—BEVERLY DANIEL TATUM, *WHY ARE ALL THE BLACK KIDS SITTING TOGETHER IN THE CAFETERIA?*

YOU AND YOUR COMMITMENTS

We are at the finish line of this book! But certainly not at the finish line of the lifelong work of antiracism. Take a moment to check in with where you are right now. How are you feeling? I imagine that many different emotions are running through you by this day, from exhaustion and heartbreak to inspiration, determination, and more. Perhaps you have more questions than answers. This is normal. When our perceptions have been expanded to see things we have never seen before, it is normal to want to re-create a feeling of stability and certainty by finding some clear and solid answers. Understanding the burden of white privilege and what it means to be personally complicit in the system of white supremacy is a lot to hold.

Holding that burden and really being with that truth is an important part of the work that people with white privilege must do. BIPOC have been holding the burden of what it feels like to be oppressed and marginalized their whole lives and back through their ancestry for generations. The devastation, anger, and confusion you are feeling are part of the work too. Without those feelings, nothing changes, because there is no reason to heal what does not feel broken.

I invite you not to run away from the pain but to allow it to break your heart open. Superficial attempts to heal racism, like color blindness, tokenism, and white saviorism, protect you from having to feel this pain. Doing the inner work and going into the truth blasts away all the lies and games, giving you a real opportunity to create change. There is no safety in this work. There is no clean, comfortable, or convenient way to dismantle a violent system of oppression. You must roll up your sleeves and get down into the ugly, fertile dirt.

What you have uncovered over the last twenty-seven days can no longer be hidden again. You cannot go back to sleep. You cannot unsee and unknow what you now see and know. And if you were to choose to do so, you would be worse off than when you began this work on Day 1.

Now that we have come to the end of this book, the question is, how are you going to stay committed from Day 29 onward? This question is actually one I want you to consider revisiting on a daily basis, because all the learning and aha moments in the world do not mean anything if they are not followed through with committed actions for change.

Two days ago, we looked at your values, and yesterday, we looked at what you are willing to lose in terms of privilege. Today, we are looking at what commitments you are ready to make to practice lifelong antiracism.

Please note that I am not talking about making promises. You cannot make promises that you will inevitably break. And you will break them, because to be human is to make mistakes, to forget, and to want to revert back to what is known, safe, and comfortable (and white privilege is a great source of comfort and safety). But what you can do is pledge commitments and take actions on those commitments. And you can repledge daily and take actions daily. So even when you slip up, forget, and regress into old white supremacist habits and behaviors, you can repledge to your commitments and begin again. Antiracism is not about perfectionism. It is about the intention to help create change met with the consistent commitment to keep learning, keep showing up, and keep doing what is necessary so that BIPOC can live with dignity and equality.

Reflective Journaling Prompts

1. Write three concrete, out-of-your-comfort-zone actions you are committed to taking in the next two weeks toward antiracism.

   These could be uncomfortable conversations you need to have, significant changes in your life you need to make, someone you need to call out/in, sincere apologies you need to make, announcements you need to make, organizations you need to begin volunteering at, etc. Make these actions as *specific* as possible (what, where, when, how, who, why, etc.) and also make clear how you will be held accountable for these actions (e.g., choose and notify an accountability partner).

2. Starting today and over the next week, begin to write down your commitments to this work.

   Craft a commitments statement that you will be able to refer to every day and especially on the days when you forget, make mistakes, or begin to slip back into white apathy. Your commitments are not what you will *try* to do or *hope* to do but what you *will* do.

   To craft this document, go back through all the days of this work and recall the ways you have done harm and the ways in which you are committed to change. Think about what you are ready to commit to in your personal life, your family life, your friendships, your work and business life, and your community life.

   Use any or all of the following writing prompts to help you craft your commitment statement:

   * *I am committed to showing up for this lifelong antiracism work because...*

- *I am committed to challenging my white fragility by…*
- *I am committed to using my voice for antiracism work by…*
- *I am committed to challenging racism in other people with white privilege by…*
- *I am committed to uplifting, supporting, and centering BIPOC by…*
- *I am committed to financially supporting the following BIPOC movements and causes…*
- *I am committed to decentering myself as a person with white privilege by…*
- *I am committed to continuing my lifelong antiracism education by…*
- *I am committed to the following values that will help me to practice antiracism…*
- *I am committed to breaking through my white apathy by…*
- *I am committed to showing up even when I make mistakes by…*
- *I am committed to using my privilege for antiracism by…*
- *I am committed to challenging my optical allyship by…*
- *I am committed to being a good ancestor by…*

Commitments are strong statements of solidarity and action. They are not guarantees that you will actually do the work, but they will help focus you so you know what work you are supposed to be doing. Commit to this lifelong work. Write it down and then live your life accordingly.

To ensure that your commitment statement does not become a symbolic document that pays lip service but does not follow through with action, keep it somewhere where you will be able to see it every day. Do not just leave it in your journal. Post it up in your home and/or workspace where you will be able to access it every day and be reminded of what you are committed to. If working through this book with family members or coworkers, consider creating a family or organizational commitment statement too.

To create accountability, share your commitment statement with a person or persons in your life who are also committed to social change and antiracism work. Keep one another accountable to showing up in the ways that you have committed to. Do not let one another slip back into the behaviors we have explored in this book.

———————————

Remember: You do not have to write it all down today. Begin today but continue this over the coming days, weeks, months, and years. Your commitment statement is not a solid document set in stone. Treat it as a living, breathing, evolving, and ever-deepening statement that reflects your own growth in this work and your commitment to antiracism as a lifelong practice.

There is no end
To what a living world
Will demand of you.

Earthseed: The Books of the Living I,
Verse 21; Octavia Butler, *Parable of the Sower*

now what?

CONTINUING THE WORK
AFTER DAY 28

After twenty-eight days of reflective journaling and inner excavation, you now have a strong foundation to continue moving forward in your practice of antiracism. In addition, you also have an extremely valuable resource—your journal of writing within which you have unpacked each day's prompts. Your writing has revealed to you what you needed to see about your personal complicity and relationship with white supremacy. What do you do with this journal?

Keep it with you, and refer to it again and again when you need to reexamine how white supremacy shows up for you. Also recognize that this journal gave you a first layer of revelations. There are many more layers to go. As your awareness has now expanded to become more conscious of *how* (and not *if*) racism is at play, you will see even more how white supremacy plays out within you and within society. To get to these deeper layers and to unpack even further, buy yourself a new journal, and when you are ready, begin the twenty-eight days again. Use this book as a resource for you to take responsibility for doing your own work. See it as a tool in your metaphorical antiracism backpack.

TIPS TO SUPPORT YOU IN CONTINUING TO DO YOUR WORK

- Return to the reflective journal prompts again and again, as needed. Go deeper each time. Dig out more so that you can do less harm.

- Seek out antiracist educators and teachers. Attend their classes, courses, workshops, and events. Self-reflecting is important, but it is not enough. Put yourself in spaces where you can learn directly from antiracist educators.

- Make curating your antiracism education and following through on your actions your responsibility. Find articles, podcasts, books, publications, and other resources to expand your understanding of historic and present-time oppression. Make lifelong learning about antiracism one of your values. Check out the Resources section at the end of this book as a starting place.

- Show up at meetings, rallies, marches, and fund-raisers for BIPOC. Show up, period.

- Financially support organizations, nonprofits, and political candidates who are working hard for BIPOC rights.

- Uplift, center, pay, and elevate BIPOC leaders and teachers.

- Uphold your commitments to living your life with integrity for your antiracist values. Live these commitments daily.

MOVING FROM THE PERSONAL TO THE SYSTEMIC

This internal work you have been doing of examining, reflecting, changing, and acting differently is just one prong in the work to dismantle white supremacy. For real change to happen, you must also challenge systems and work to create structural changes, dismantling white supremacy institutionally as well as personally. It is hard to imagine what a world without white supremacy would be like. A world where BIPOC get to live with the same level of dignity and humanity as white people. And yet we must continue to work toward it. White supremacy is the paradigm we have come to accept as normal. But normal does not make it right. It never has.

Even though this personal antiracism work is just one prong of the dismantling of white supremacy, it is incredibly important. Systems do not change unless the people who uphold them change, and each person is responsible for upholding the system. So it is your responsibility within yourself, your communities, your educational institutions, your corporations, and your government institutions to do the work that you *can* do every day to create the change the world needs by creating change within yourself.

A FINAL NOTE

I began this book by telling you about my purpose, which is to become a good ancestor. To leave this world in a better place than I found it, for my children and for everyone else who is and who will be impacted by my being here on the planet today. As we close up our time together, I want to speak to the good ancestor who lies within you, the person inside you who came to this book with questions about dismantling white supremacy and who leaves this book knowing that *you* are a part of the problem and that you are *simultaneously* also a part of the answer. There is great power and responsibility in that knowledge. But knowledge without action is meaningless.

To dismantle this system of oppression and marginalization that has hurt so many for so many generations, we need all of us. In creating a new world, everyone's contribution matters. And as someone who holds white privilege, your contribution to this work is of the utmost importance. No matter who you are, you have the power to influence change in the world. The effects of your actions, whether consciously chosen or not, will impact everyone who comes into contact with you and what you create in the world while you are alive. You can continue to unconsciously allow white supremacy to use you as it used your ancestors, to cause an impact of harm and marginalization to BIPOC. Or you can intentionally choose to disrupt and dismantle white supremacy within yourself and your communities so that BIPOC can live free of racism and oppression.

The choice is yours. The moment is now.

Help change the world. Become a good ancestor.

appendix

WORKING IN GROUPS: *ME AND WHITE SUPREMACY* BOOK CIRCLES

When I initially created and ran the #MeAndWhiteSupremacy challenge, I did not know that it would go viral. I did not know that I would eventually turn it into a free workbook or that it would eventually become this book that you are holding your hands. I did not know that there would be great demand from people wanting to know how to work through these reflective journaling questions in family, community, academic, and workplace settings. While writing this book, one of the questions that arose again and again was "Will there be instructions for how to go through the book in a group?"

When the twenty-eight-day challenge was originally conceived, it was specifically designed as a personal, self-reflection activity. As I sat with the question of how to make this personal work translatable into a group setting, I knew that I did not want to reinvent the wheel. I did not want to have to design a completely new process. So instead I went out looking for a process that could work with the book. As part of my investigations, I knew I wanted to find a process that was:

- Time-tested

- Nonhierarchical

- Structured yet flexible

- Capable of being used whether groups were big or small, intimate or businesslike, virtual or in-person

- Simple and easy to implement yet powerful

It was very important to me that the process I recommended for group settings would not perpetuate oppressive power dynamics by design. It was also very important to me that the process be one that I would personally find value in taking part in and be comfortable recommending. In researching ways to have conversations regarding white supremacy, I came across the work of Christina Baldwin and Ann Linnea called The Circle Way. Now retired, they have carefully passed their life work into a collective found online at thecircleway.net. Under the Creative Commons Attribution 3 License on this website and with their kind permission, I have included basic information for using the principles and practices of The Circle Way.

WHAT IS THE CIRCLE WAY?

The Circle Way is a structure for deep conversation and wise outcomes based on a methodology founded by Christina Baldwin and Ann Linnea in 1992 and fully expounded upon in their 2010 book, *The Circle Way: A Leader in Every Chair*. Baldwin and Linnea describe The Circle Way as a process that gathers people into a circular shape with participants at the rim and the purpose in the center. Each person has a voice, and everyone can see and hear one another. Social agreements and practices help facilitate respectful conversation. The process is simple to use yet powerful in its impact. The process of The Circle Way is nonhierarchical and supports a leader in every chair. Everyone who is part of the circle is responsible for holding the structure, energy, and purpose of the circle.

In addition, The Circle Way lends itself well to antiracism practice and racial justice change. The Circle Way website states that "in light of these times, The Circle Way reaffirms the essential practice of taking a seat on the rim and turning to one another to uphold racial, ethnic, gender, economic, and environmental justice."[55]

The Circle Way book explains that "we have the opportunity in circle process to heal our old stories and to make new stories that lead to different actions and create a different world. This is the essential task of our times! Understanding the power of story and the container of the circle give us life skills that have profoundly transformational potential. We can talk the world we need into being and then align our actions with our vision. This is what our ancestors did at the fire, and if we are to become ancestors to future generations, this is what we will do today."[56]

WHY DO YOU NEED TO USE A PARTICULAR PROCESS FOR WORKING THROUGH THIS BOOK IN GROUPS?

It is important to me that people working through this book have the ability to do so in group settings if they wish to do so. However, there are a lot of risks involved when leaving the format of how these groups should be facilitated to chance. If left to chance, it is highly likely that the white supremacist behaviors discussed in this book start to run the show.

Without clear guidance, instruction, and structure, the following could occur:

- No clear intention or purpose for coming together as a group.

- No clear structure for holding the conversation, where everyone gets to speak with equal time and focus.

- No clear agreements and guidelines for what will and will not be permitted during group meetings, leading to potential chaos through white fragility, white centering, white exceptionalism, etc.

- A hierarchical structure forms where some people in the group are able to dominate over others if they are louder, more forceful, seen as "further ahead" in the work, etc.

- Lack of focus and structure leads to distraction, derailing, and the meeting simply becoming a social get-together.

- Not being clear on the intention of the group, therefore having certain members in the group who are not ready or willing to do the work, thus undermining the purpose of coming together in the group in the first place.

- All of the above and more leading to the *Me and White Supremacy* work being minimized, tokenized, undermined, and ultimately wasted.

It is for these reasons that I ask that the recommended format to do the *Me and White Supremacy* work in a group is through The Circle Way.

If a *Me and White Supremacy* book circle is something you truly want to host, the best place to go for a comprehensive guide is *The Circle Way* book. The book will answer most of the questions you have about how to design and run a *Me and White Supremacy* book circle.

However, you do not need to read the entire book to host a circle. The authors of the book and founders of the process have generously created many free and paid resources on The Circle Way website. On the Resources page of the website, you will find books, videos, The Circle Way guidelines (which, at the time of writing this book, are available in fourteen languages), questions about circle, booklets (including the very useful *The Circle Way Pocket Guide*), case-study stories and tips, learning maps, and articles. With these resources, you will be well equipped to understand how The Circle Way works and how to design a *Me and White Supremacy* book circle based on The Circle Way process.

THE CIRCLE WAY GUIDELINES

For the purpose of clarity, I am including a brief outline of the basic guidelines of The Circle Way process. These guidelines are excerpted from the books *Calling the Circle: The First and Future Culture* by Christina Baldwin and *The Circle Way*. The following excerpt and circle diagram were taken from The Circle Way guidelines that can be found on the website. The basic Circle Way guidelines PDF condenses the art of hosting a circle into a two-page, easy-to-understand document. I recommend downloading the document itself and studying all the resources on The Circle Way website to gain even more clarity and understanding on how The Circle Way works. Christina Baldwin and Ann Linnea have generously created a plethora of resources to help you understand and use the circle process.

If your wishes as a group host and/or participant are to truly honor the work I am offering through this book, then please go through all the available materials carefully and thoroughly to ensure that you create the best space possible for doing this work.

I appreciate The Circle Way's spirit of generosity in allowing people access to their information and practice. Its inclusion here does not indicate endorsement. Readers are encouraged to explore The Circle Way website to find other open materials and to read the book, *The Circle Way: A Leader in Every Chair*.

EXCERPTED FROM "THE CIRCLE WAY: BASIC GUIDELINES FOR CALLING A CIRCLE"

Components of Circle

What transforms a meeting into a circle is the willingness of people to shift from informal socializing or opinionated discussion into a receptive attitude of thoughtful speaking and deep listening that embodies the practices and structures outlined here.

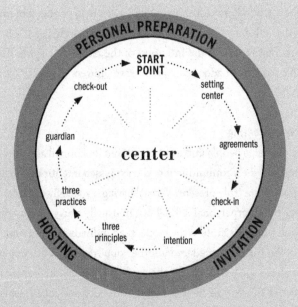

Intention

Intention shapes the circle and determines who will come, how long the circle will meet, and what kinds of outcomes are to be expected. The caller of the circle spends time articulating intention and invitation.

Start-Point or Welcome

Once people have gathered, it is helpful for the host, or a volunteer participant, to begin the circle with a gesture that shifts people's attention from social space to council space. This gesture of welcome may be a moment of silence, reading a poem, or listening to a song—whatever invites centering.

Setting the Center

The center of a circle is like the hub of a wheel: all energies pass through it, and it holds the rim together. To help people remember how the hub helps the group, the center of a circle usually holds objects that represent the intention of the circle. Any symbol that fits this purpose or adds beauty will serve: flowers, a bowl or basket, a candle.

Check-In/Greeting

Check-in helps people into a frame of mind for council and reminds everyone of their commitment to the expressed intention. It insures that people are truly present. Verbal sharing, especially a brief story, weaves the interpersonal net. Check-in usually starts with a volunteer and proceeds around the circle. If an individual is not ready to speak, the turn is passed and another opportunity is offered after others have spoken. Sometimes people place individual objects in the center as a way of signifying their presence and relationship to the intention.

Guardian

The single most important tool for aiding self-governance and bringing circle back to intention is the role of guardian. One circle member volunteers to watch and safeguard group energy and observe the circle's process. The guardian usually employs a gentle noisemaker, such as a chime, bell, or rattle, that signals to everyone to stop action, take a breath, rest in a space of silence. The guardian makes this signal again and speaks to why s/he called the pause. Any member may call for a pause.

Setting Circle Agreements

The use of agreements allows all members to have a free and profound exchange, to respect a diversity of views, and to share responsibility for the well-being and direction of the group.

Agreements often used include:

* We hold all stories or personal material in confidentiality.

* We listen to one another with compassion and curiosity.

* We ask for what we need and offer what we can.

* We agree to employ a group guardian to watch our needs, timing, and energy.

* We agree to pause at a signal when we feel the need to pause.

Three Principles

1. Leadership rotates among all circle members.
2. Responsibility is shared for the quality of experience.
3. Reliance is on wholeness, rather than on any personal agenda.

Three Practices

1. Speak with intention: noting what has relevance to the conversation in the moment.
2. Listen with attention: respectful of the learning process for all members of the group.
3. Tend to the well-being of the circle: remaining aware of the impact of our contributions.

Forms of Council

1. Talking piece council is often used as a part of check-in, check-out, and whenever there is a desire to slow down the conversation, collect all voices and contributions, and be able to speak without interruption.
2. Conversation council is often used when reaction, interaction, and an interjection of new ideas, thoughts, and opinions are needed.
3. Reflection, or silent council, gives each member time and space to reflect on what is occurring, or needs to occur, in the course of a meeting. Silence may be called so that each person can consider the role or impact they are having on the group, or to help the group realign with their intention, or to sit with a question until there is clarity.

Check-Out and Farewell

At the close of a circle meeting, it is important to allow a few minutes for each person to comment on what they learned, or what stays in their heart and mind as they leave. Closing the circle by checking out provides a formal end to the meeting, a chance for members to reflect on what has transpired, and to pick up objects if they have placed something in the center.

As people shift from council space to social space or private time, they release each other from the intensity of attention being in circle requires. Often after check-out, the host, guardian, or a volunteer will offer a few inspirational words of farewell, or signal a few seconds of silence before the circle is released.

IMPORTANT CONSIDERATIONS FOR WHEN YOU ARE READY TO CREATE AND RUN A *ME AND WHITE SUPREMACY* CIRCLE

- Before making any announcements to create a group, go through all the aforementioned resources and study them thoroughly. Understand the basic guidelines and structure of the process before taking any outward action.

- Clarify your intention and stated purpose for the circle. Do not leave it to chance. Write out your stated purpose and keep it front and center at every meeting.

- Use discernment and intention to invite the right members to be in the circle with. Not everybody is willing to do this work. Not everyone is willing to follow the structure of the circle or set aside white fragility to be a part of something bigger. Make sure the people you are inviting to be in the circle are ready to really do the work.

- Decide on your format for the circle—will it be in person or virtual? While The Circle Way is described in terms of a physical, in-person circle, I have taken part in circles run over virtual software that follow The Circle Way process. With the right intentionality and focus, it can be done well.

- Other considerations:
  - How frequently will the circle meet?
  - When and where will you meet?
  - Will you cover one journaling day per meeting or group days together and cover a few per meeting?
  - How long will the meeting be?
  - How many minutes will each person get during the talking piece council portion of the meeting?
  - Will you be journaling during the meetings or only talking about what you have journaled on prior to the meeting?

- Think carefully about the entire format of the circle. It is important to do as much preparation work as possible up front so that when you are in circle time, things run smoothly, expectations are clear, and the impact is powerful.

- Make very clear agreements for the circle. In *The Circle Way Pocket Guide* (which can also be found for free on The Circle Way website), agreements are described as providing an "interpersonal safety net for participation in the conversations that are about to occur. In a circle, where you're practicing rotating leadership and shared responsibility, agreements tell people what they can expect from each other and what is likely to happen in the exchanges between them." Make clear agreements on how the circle will be run, what behavior will and will not be permitted, how you will challenge each other to go deeper in the work, how you will respect each other's boundaries, etc. Be as specific as possible. Up-front agreements before beginning the work can help to minimize the risks of derailment and chaos I mentioned earlier.

- Be intentional and consistent about following the three principles (rotating leadership, shared responsibility, and reliance on wholeness), and the three practices (intentional speaking, attentive listening, and tending the well-being of the circle) of The Circle Way.

- Have clear roles assigned for each meeting, with clarity on who is the host, guardian, and scribe each time.

- Do not let the circle unravel into simply a social circle and time to spend with your friends. Come together with intention, hold the intention each time you meet, and do not get distracted or sidetracked.

- Do not become apathetic or self-congratulatory in the circle. Do not allow white fragility to take over.

- Understand that even with all these checks and balances in place, it is still possible for white supremacist behaviors to sneak in (centering, dominance, fragility, etc.). Work hard to challenge these within yourself and one another. This is also part of the work.

- Understand that whether you have an assigned role or not in the circle, each circle member is a leader. Take responsibility. Do not leave the success of the circle to one or two people. Work together as a group to ensure the best possible outcome, with the best possible outcome being that in doing this work, you show up better for BIPOC.

FAQS

Can we charge people to attend *Me and White Supremacy* book circles?

No facilitators hosting *Me and White Supremacy* book circles should use the circles to make a profit. However, it is okay to charge attendees to cover the costs of location if the circle is being held at a location that requires a fee. Ticket prices should be to cover costs only and not to cover time or energy spent in hosting or facilitating the circle.

Can we ask BIPOC to join *Me and White Supremacy* book circles with us?

This work takes a considerable emotional labor toll on BIPOC, and the work is not for them to do—it is for people with white privilege to do. If BIPOC want to attend the circle, they may do so. However, they should not be expected to do the journaling work, support the emotional processing, or be called upon to teach or explain if they do not wish to do so. Ideally, they should be there as observers, and clear boundaries and policies should be put in place to ensure that they do not perform emotional labor and are not harmed through racial aggressions.

Can we hire BIPOC to host *Me and White Supremacy* book circles to keep us accountable?

As the *Me and White Supremacy* process is protected intellectual property, it is not permissible to hire anyone except Layla Saad or anyone licensed by Layla Saad to lead the process. The Circle Way is not a process that requires a leader but rather one that supports a leader in every chair. No hired facilitator is required for hosting a *Me and White Supremacy* book circle.

resources

GLOSSARY

AAVE: African American Vernacular English.

Ally Cookies: Praise or other rewards for "not being racist." Usually sought out by people with white privilege performing optical allyship.

Anti-Blackness: Defined by *Merriam-Webster* as being opposed to or hostile toward Black people. Anti-Blackness or anti-Black racism can be found all around the world.

BIPOC: Black, Indigenous, and People of Color.

BIWOC: Black, Indigenous, and Women of Color.

Blackface: Wearing dark makeup to caricature a Black person. Its origins can be found in American minstrel shows of the nineteenth century where white actors wore dark face paint to depict racist caricatures of enslaved and free Black people on stage.

Blackfishing: The use of artificial tanning and makeup by people with white privilege to make their skin look darker and give the impression that they are of African descent. A modern form of blackface.

Cisgender: A term for people whose gender identity matches the biological sex they were assigned at birth.

The Circle Way: A structure for deep conversation and wise outcomes based on a methodology founded by Christina Baldwin and Ann Linnea in 1992 and fully expounded upon in their 2010 book, *The Circle Way: A Leader in Every Chair.* The Circle Way is the preferred and recommended structure and methodology that *Me and White Supremacy* book circles should follow for working through *Me and White Supremacy* in group settings.

Colorism: A term coined by author Alice Walker in her book *In Search of our Mothers' Gardens.* Walker defined colorism as the "prejudicial or preferential treatment of same-race people based solely on their color."[57] Colorism is where prejudicial treatment is given to darker-skinned Black people and People of Color and preferential treatment is given to lighter-skinned Black people and People of Color.

Cultural Appropriation: A modern type of colonization that involves the appropriation and sometimes commercialization of cultural practices, spiritual traditions, hair and dress fashion styles, speaking styles, and other cultural elements. Cultural appropriation happens when there is an imbalance of power and privilege—a dominant or privileged culture appropriates from a nondominant or marginalized culture. Cultural appropriation does not work the other way around. BIPOC cannot appropriate from white people, because BIPOC do not hold collective power and privilege over white people.

Digital Blackface: In the digital world, the use of emojis, GIFs, and memes featuring Black people by people who hold white privilege.

Intersectionality: A term coined by law professor and civil rights advocate Dr. Kimberlé Crenshaw. It is a framework that helps us to explore the dynamic between coexisting identities and connected systems of oppression, particularly as it relates to gender and race and the experiences of Black women.

Me and White Supremacy **Book Circle:** Based on The Circle Way, this is the preferred and recommended structure and methodology for working through the *Me and White Supremacy* book in group settings.

Misogynoir: A term coined by African American feminist scholar, writer, and activist Moya Bailey to describe misogyny directed specifically toward Black women. The intersection of sexism and anti-Black racism.

Optical Allyship: The visual illusion of allyship without the actual work of allyship. Also known as *performative allyship* or *ally theatre*.

Tokenism: Defined by Oxford Dictionaries as "the practice of making only a perfunctory or symbolic effort to do a particular thing, especially by recruiting a small number of people from underrepresented groups in order to give the appearance of sexual or racial equality within a workforce."[58]

Tone Policing: A tactic used by those who have white privilege to silence those who do not by focusing on the tone of what is being said rather than the actual content. Tone policing does not only have to be spoken out loud publicly. People with white privilege often tone police BIPOC in their thoughts or behind closed doors.

Voluntourism: The trend and business of volunteer tourism, where people with privilege from Western countries travel to do charity volunteer work in countries across Africa, Asia, and Latin America. Voluntourism has been criticized for perpetuating white saviorism.

White Apathy: A feeling of apathy, indifference, unconcern, detachment, dispassion, and disregard about racism by people with white privilege.

White Centering: The centering of whiteness and white people, white values, white norms, and white feelings over everything and everyone else. The belief, whether conscious or not, that whiteness is "normal" and BIPOC are "other."

White Exceptionalism: The belief that people with white privilege are exempt from white supremacy. The belief of being "one of the good ones."

White Feminism: A feminism that focuses on the struggle of white women. It is feminism that is only concerned with disparities and oppression of gender (usually cisgender) but does not take into account disparities and oppression of other intersections that are just as important, including race, class, age, ability, sexual orientation, gender identity, etc.

White Fragility: A phrase coined by author Robin DiAngelo, defined as "a state in which even a minimum amount of racial stress becomes intolerable, triggering a range of defensive moves."[59]

White Gaze: The white supremacist lens through which people with white privilege see BIPOC. The white gaze also describes how BIPOC are defined, limited, stereotyped, and judged in the white imagination, usually to the detriment of BIPOC.

White Privilege: A phrase coined by Peggy McIntosh in her 1988 paper "White Privilege and Male Privilege: A Personal Account of Coming to See Correspondences Through Work in Women's Studies" and defined as follows: "I have come to see white privilege as an invisible package of unearned assets that I can count on cashing in each day, but about which I was 'meant' to remain oblivious. White privilege is like an invisible weightless knapsack of special provisions, assurances, tools, maps, guides, codebooks, passports, visas, clothes, compass, emergency gear, and blank checks."[60]

White Saviorism: A colonialist idea that assumes that BIPOC need white people to save them, that without white intervention, instruction, and guidance, BIPOC will be left helpless, and that without whiteness, BIPOC, who are seen and treated as inferior to people with white privilege, will not survive.

White Silence: Occurs when people with white privilege stay complicity silent when it comes to issues of race.

White Superiority: The erroneous, violent, and racist idea that people with white or white-passing skin are superior to and therefore deserve to dominate over people with brown or black skin.

FURTHER LEARNING

Antiracism is a lifelong practice that requires constant and consistent self-education. Below is a nonexhaustive list of resources and teachers who can support you on your journey.

BOOKS

Adegoke, Yomi and Uviebginené. *Slay in Your Lane: The Black Girl Bible*. London: Fourth Estate, 2018.

Akala. *Natives: Race and Class in the Ruins of Empire*. London: Two Roads, 2018.

Alexander, Michelle. *The New Jim Crow: Mass Incarceration in the Age of Colorblindness*. New York: The New Press, 2012.

Anderson, Carol. *White Rage: The Unspoken Truth of Our Racial Divide*. New York: Bloomsbury, 2017.

Baldwin, Christina, and Ann Linnea. *The Circle Way Pocket Guide*. The Circle Way, 2016.

Baldwin, James. *The Fire Next Time*. New York: The Dial Press, 1963.

Banaji, Mahzarin R. and Anthony G. Greenwald. *Blindspot: Hidden Biases of Good People*. New York: Bantam Books, 2016.

Bhopal, Kalwant. *White Privilege: The Myth of a Post-racial Society*. Bristol: Policy Press, 2018.

Bonilla-Silva, Eduardo. *Racism without Racists: Color-Blind Racism and the Persistence of Racial Inequality in America*. 5th ed. Lanham, MD: Rowman & Littlefield, 2018.

Brathwaite, Candice. *I Am Not Your Baby Mother*. London: Quercus, a division of Hachette UK, 2020.

brown, adrienne maree. *Emergent Strategy: Shaping Change, Changing Worlds*. Reprint edition. AK Press, 2017.

Brown, Austin Channing. *I'm Still Here: Black Dignity in a World Made for Whiteness*. New York: Convergent Books, 2018.

Camahort Page, Elisa, Carolyn Gerin, and Jamia Wilson. *Road Map for Revolutionaries: Resistance, Activism, and Advocacy for All*. New York: Ten Speed Press, 2018.

Carruthers, Charlene. *Unapologetic: A Black, Queer, and Feminist Mandate for Radical Movements*. Boston: Beacon Press, 2018.

Coates, Ta-Nehisi. *Between the World and Me*. New York: Spiegel & Grau, 2015.

Cooper, Brittney. *Eloquent Rage: A Black Feminist Discovers Her Superpower*. New York: St. Martin's Press, 2018.

Crenshaw, Kimberlé. "On Intersectionality: Essential Writings." In *Critical Race Theory: The Key Writings That Formed the Movement*, edited by Kimberlé Crenshaw, Neil Gotanda, Gary Peller, and Kendall Thomas. New York: The New Press, 1996.

Dabiri, Emma. *Don't Touch My Hair*. London: Allen Lane, a division of Penguin Random House UK, 2019.

Davis, Angela Y. *Women, Race & Class*. New York: Vintage, 2983.

DeGruy, Joy. *Post Traumatic Slave Syndrome: America's Legacy of Enduring Injury and Healing*. Revised ed. Joy DeGruy Publications, 2017.

DiAngelo, Robin. *What Does It Mean to Be White?: Developing White Racial Literacy*. Revised edition. New York: Peter Lang Publishing, 2016. London: Allen Lane, a division of Penguin Random House UK, 2019.

DiAngelo, Robin. *White Fragility: Why It's So Hard for White People to Talk about Racism*. Boston: Beacon Press, 2018.

Dyson, Michael Eric. *Tears We Cannot Stop: A Sermon to White America*. New York: St. Martin's Press, 2017.

Eddo-Lodge, Reni. *Why I'm No Longer Talking to White People about Race*. London: Bloomsbury, 2017.

Fleming, Crystal Marie. *How to Be Less Stupid about Race*. Boston: Beacon Press, 2018.

gal-dem. *I Will Not Be Erased: Our Stories About Growing Up as People of Colour*. London: Walker Books, 2019.

Hirsch, Afua. *Brit(ish): On Race, Identity and Belonging*. London: Vintage Books, a division of Penguin Random House, UK, 2018.

hooks, bell. *Ain't I a Woman?: Black Women and Feminism.* New York: Routledge, 2015.

Irving, Debby. *Waking Up White, and Finding Myself in the Story of Race.* Cambridge, MA: Elephant Room Press, 2014.

Jackson, Catrice M. *Antagonist, Advocates and Allies: The Wake-Up Call Guide for White Women Who Want to Become Allies with Black Women.* Omaha, NE: Catriceology Enterprises, 2015.

Jerkins, Morgan. *This Will Be My Undoing: Living at the Intersection of Black, Female, and Feminist in (White) America.* New York: Harper Perennial, 2018.

Johnson, Michelle Cassandra. *Skill in Action: Radicalizing Your Yoga Practice to Create a Just World.* Portland, OR: Radical Transformation Media, 2017.

Jones, Feminista. *Reclaiming Our Space: How Black Feminists Are Changing the World from the Tweets to the Streets.* Boston: Beacon Press, 2019.

Jones-Rogers, Stephane E. *They Were Her Property: White Women as Slave Owners in the American South.* New Haven, CT: Yale University Press, 2019.

Kendi, Ibram X. *How to Be an Antiracist.* New York: One World, 2019. London: Bodley Head, 2019.

Kendi, Ibram X. *Stamped from the Beginning: The Definitive History of Racist Ideas in America.* New York: Nation Books, 2016. Paperback edition: London, Bodley Head, 2017.

Khan-Cullors, Patrisse, and asha bandele. *When They Call You a Terrorist: A Black Lives Matter Memoir.* Reprint ed. New York: St. Martin's Press, 2018.

Khan, Mariam. *It's Not About the Burqa: Muslim Women on Faith, Feminism, Sexuality and Race.* London: Picador, an imprint of Pan Macmillan, 2019.

Kendall, Mikki. *Hood Feminism.* London: Bloomsbury Publishing, 2020.

Lawal, Elijah. *The Clapback.* London: Hodder & Stoughton, a division of Hachette UK, 2019.

Laymon, Kiese. *Heavy: An American Memoir.* New York: Scribner, 2018.

Laymon, Kiese. *How to Slowly Kill Yourself and Others in America.* Evanston, IL: Agate Publishing, 2013.

Lorde, Audre. *Sister Outsider: Essays and Speeches.* Revised edition. New York: Ten Speed Press, 2007. First published in 1984.

Mckesson, DeRay. *On the Other Side of Freedom: The Case for Hope.* New York: Viking, 2018.

Menakem, Resmaa. *My Grandmother's Hands: Racialized Trauma and the Pathway to Mending Our Hearts and Bodies.* Las Vegas: Central Recovery Press, 2017.

Moraga, Cherríe, and Gloria Anzaldúa, eds. *This Bridge Called My Back: Writings by Radical Women of Color.* 4th ed. Albany, NY: State University of New York Press, 2015.

Morrison, Toni. *Playing in the Dark: Whiteness and the Literary Imagination.* Somerville, MA: Harvard University Press, 1992.

Noble, Safiya Umoja. *Algorithms of Oppression: How Search Engines Reinforce Racism.* New York: New York University Press, 2018.

Oluo, Ijeoma. *So You Want to Talk about Race.* New York: Hachette Book Group, 2018.

Olusoga, David. *Black and British: A Forgotten History.* London: Pan Macmillan, 2016.

Owusu, Derek. *Safe: On Black British Men Reclaiming Space.* London: Trapeze, an imprint of The Orion Publishing Group, Hachette UK, 2019.

Rankine, Claudia. *Citizen: An American Lyric.* Minneapolis: Graywolf Press, 2014.

Shukla, Nikesh. *The Good Immigrant.* London: Unbound, 2016.

Solomon, Akiba, and Kenrya Rankin. *How We Fight White Supremacy: A Field Guide to Black Resistance.* New York: Bold Type Books, 2019.

Stevenson, Bryan. *Just Mercy: A Story of Justice and Redemption.* New York: Spiegel & Grau, 2014.

Tatum, Beverly Daniel. *Why Are All the Black Kids Sitting Together in the Cafeteria?: And Other Conversations about Race.* New York: Hachette Book Group, 2017. First published in 1997 by Basic Books (New York).

Taylor, Keeanga-Yamahtta. *How We Get Free: Black Feminism and the Combahee River Collective.* Chicago: Haymarket Books, 2017.

Whytelaw, Dr Boulé III. *Think Like a White Man: Conquering the World . . . While Black.* London: Canongate, 2019.

Williams, Rev. angel Kyodo, Lama Rod Owens, and Jasmine Syedullah. *Radical Dharma: Talking Race, Love, and Liberation.* Berkeley: North Atlantic Books, 2016.

PODCASTS

brown, adrienne maree and Autumn Brown. *How to Survive the End of the World.* https://www.endoftheworldshow.org/.

Crenshaw, Kimberlé. *Intersectionality Matters!* http://aapf.org/podcast.

Eddo-Lodge, Reni. *About Race.* https://www.aboutracepodcast.com/.

Kelly, Kerri. *CTZN Podcast.* http://www.ctznwell.org/ctznpodcast.

Mckesson, DeRay, with Brittany Packnett, Sam Sinyangwe, and Clint Smith. *Pod Save the People.* https://crooked.com/podcast-series/ pod-save-the-people/.

Moore, EbonyJanice. *Black Girl Mixtape.* https://www.blackgirl-mixtape.com/.

Rye, Angela. *On One with Angela Rye.* https://podcasts.apple.com/us/podcast /on-one-with-angela-rye/id1257985728.

Saad, Layla F. *Good Ancestor Podcast*. http://laylafsaad.com/good-ancestor-podcast.

Scene on Radio. *Seeing White*. https://www.sceneonradio.org/seeing-white/.

Wilbur, Matika and Adrienne Keene. *All My Relations Podcast*. https://www.allmy relationspodcast.com/.

FILMS AND DOCUMENTARIES

Burns, Ken, Sarah Burns, and David McMahon, dirs. *The Central Park Five*. Sundance Selects, Florentine Films, and PBS, 2012. DVD, 119 min.

DuVernay, Ava, dir. *13th*. Kandoo Films, Forward Movement, 2016. Netflix.

DuVernay, Ava, dir. *When They See Us*. Tribeca Productions, Array, and Participant Media, 2019. Netflix.

Peck, Raoul, dir. *I Am Not Your Negro*. Velvet Film, Artemis Productions, and Close Up Films, 2016 (2017, United States). DVD.

Shannon, Lyttanya, dir. *The Naked Truth*. Season 2, episode 2, "Death by Delivery." Aired March 8, 2017, on Fusion TV.

Vargas, Jose Antonion, dir. *White People*. MTV, 2015. https://www.youtube.com /watch?v=_zjj1PmJcRM.

Wah, Lee Mun, dir. *The Color of Fear*. 1994. DVD.

notes

1   Wikipedia, s.v. "White Supremacy," last modified May 8, 2019, 18:29, https://en.wikipedia
    .org/wiki/White_supremacy.

2   Peggy McIntosh, "White Privilege and Male Privilege: A Personal Account of Coming
    to See Correspondences through Work in Women's Studies," College Art, 1988, https://
    www.collegeart.org/pdf/diversity/white-privilege-and-male-privilege.pdf.

3   Natalie Angier, "Do Races Differ? Not Really, Genes Show," New York Times, August 22,
    2000, https://www.nytimes.com/2000/08/22/science/do-races-differ-not-really-genes
    -show.html.

4   McIntosh, "White Privilege and Male Privilege."

5   Robin DiAngelo, White Fragility: Why It's So Hard for White People to Talk about Racism
    (Boston: Beacon Press, 2018), 103.

6   Layla F. Saad, "I Need to Talk to Spiritual White Women about White Supremacy (Part
    One)," blog post, August 15, 2007, http://laylafsaad.com/poetry-prose/white-women
    -white-supremacy-1.

7   Furqan Mohamed, "Serena Williams: A Case Study in Misogynoir," Teen Eye Magazine,
    September 17, 2018, http://www.teeneyemagazine.com/5583952be4b08f78c1dda44d
    /2018/9/9/serena-williams-a-case-study-in-misogynoir.

8   Crystal Fleming, "Serena Williams: The Greatest Player of All Time and A Classic Case
    of Misogynoir," Newsweek, September 13, 2018, https://www.newsweek.com/serena
    -williams-greatest-player-all-time-and-classic-case-misogynoir-opinion-1119510.

9   Claudia Rankine, Citizen: An American Lyric (Minneapolis: Gray Wolf Press, 2014), 32.

10 Stephanie A. Sarkis, "11 Warning Signs of Gaslighting," Psychology Today, January 22, 2017,
    https://www.psychologytoday.com/us/blog/here-there-and-everywhere/201701/11

-warning-signs-gaslighting; Nina Porzucki, "Here's Where 'Gaslighting' Got Its Name," *The World*, Public Radio International, October 14, 2016, https://www.pri.org/stories/2016 -10-14/heres-where-gaslighting-got-its-name.

11   *Merriam-Webster*, s.v. "superior (*adj.*)," accessed June 2, 2019, http://unabridged.merriam -webster.com/collegiate/superior.

12   "LDF Celebrates the 60th Anniversary of Brown v. Board of Education: The Significance of 'The Doll Test,'" NAACP Legal Defense and Education Fund, accessed June 2, 2019, https://www.naacpldf.org/ldf-celebrates-60th-anniversary-brown-v-board-education /significance-doll-test/.

13   "Study: White and Black Children Biased Toward Lighter Skin," CNN, May 14, 2010, http://edition.cnn.com/2010/US/05/13/doll.study/index.html.

14   Dr. Martin Luther King Jr., "Letter from a Birmingham Jail," April 16, 1963, https:// kinginstitute.stanford.edu/king-papers/documents/letter-birmingham-jail.

15   Ellen Pence, "Racism—A White Issue," in *All the Women Are White, All the Blacks Are Men, But Some of Us Are Brave*, ed. Akasha (Gloria T.) Hull, Patricia Bell Scott, and Barbara Smith (New York: The Feminist Press, 1982).

16   Eduardo Bonilla-Silva, *Racism Without Racists: Color-Blind Racism and the Persistence of Racial Inequality in Contemporary America*, 3rd ed. (Lanham, MD: Rowman & Littlefield, 2010), 1.

17   Bonilla-Silva, *Racism without Racists*, 1.

18   *Merriam-Webster*, s.v. "antiblack (*adj.*)," accessed June 3, 2019, http://unabridged.merriam -webster.com/collegiate/antiblack; the Movement for Black Lives Glossary, s.v. "anti-Black racism," accessed June 3, 2019, https://policy.m4bl.org/glossary/.

19   Kirsten Chuba, "Viola Davis Proclaims 'I Cannot Lead with Bull—' at *Hollywood Reporter* Women in Entertainment Event," *Hollywood Reporter*, December 5, 2018, https:// www.hollywoodreporter.com/news/viola-davis-proclaims-i-cannot-lead-bull-thr-wie -2018-1166333.

20   Melissa V. Harris-Perry, *Sister Citizen: Shame, Stereotypes, and Black Women in America* (New Haven, CT: Yale University Press, 2011).

21   https://graziadaily.co.uk/life/opinion/black-british-women-understand-pain-americas- race-problems/
https://www.theguardian.com/commentisfree/2018/jul/20/strong-black-woman- stereotype-mental-health-depression-self-harm
https://www.bbc.co.uk/sounds/play/b0b9zfws

22   https://www.npeu.ox.ac.uk/downloads/files/mbrrace-uk/reports/MBRRACE-UK%20 Maternal%20Report%202018%20-%20Web%20Version.pdf

23   "Pregnancy Mortality Surveillance System," Centers for Disease Control and Prevention, August 7, 2018, https://www.cdc.gov/reproductivehealth/maternalinfanthealth/pregnancy -mortality-surveillance-system.htm.

24   Harris-Perry, *Sister Citizen*, 71.

25   Moya Bailey, "They Aren't Talking about Me," *Crunk Feminist Collection* (blog), March 14, 2010, http://www.crunkfeministcollective.com/2010/03/14/they-arent-talking-about-me/.

26   Jason Hanna, Kristina Sgueglia, and Darran Simon, "The Men Arrested at Starbucks Are Paying It Forward Big Time," CNN, May 3, 2018, https://www.cnn.com/2018/05/03/us/starbucks-arrest-agreements/index.html.

27   Wikipedia, s.v. "Magical Negro," last modified May 25, 2019, 20:10, https://en.wikipedia.org/wiki/Magical_Negro.

28   Philip Goff et al., "The Essence of Innocence: Consequences of Dehumanizing Black Children," *Journal of Personality and Social Psychology* 106, no. 4 (2014): 526–545.

29   Rebecca Epstein, Jamilia J. Blake, and Thalia González, "Girlhood Interrupted: The Erasure of Black Girls' Childhood," Georgetown Law Center on Poverty and Inequality, June 27, 2017, https://www.law.georgetown.edu/poverty-inequality-center/wp-content/uploads/sites/14/2017/08/girlhood-interrupted.pdf.

30   Epstein, Blake, and González, "Girlhood Interrupted."

31   David Moye, "Black Texas Teenager Brutalized in 2015 Finally Gets Her Pool Party," *Huffington Post*, June 20, 2018, https://www.huffingtonpost.ca/entry/dajerria-becton-pool-party-viral-video_n_5b2a751be4b0a4dc99233e9d.

32   For a further breakdown of these groups, see Robin DiAngelo, *What Does It Mean to Be White? Developing White Racial Literacy* (New York: Peter Lang, 2012), especially Chapter 15, "Racism and Specific Racial Groups."

33   Ijeoma Oluo, *So You Want to Talk about Race* (New York: Seal Press, 2018), 134.

34   "What Is Allyship? Why Can't I Be an Ally?" PeerNetBC, November 22, 2016, http://www.peernetbc.com/what-is-allyship.

35   *Merriam-Webster*, s.v. "apathy (*n.*)," accessed June 3, 2019, http://unabridged.merriam-webster.com/collegiate/apathy.

36   Sameer Rao, "#TBT to When Toni Morrison Checked Charlie Rose on White Privilege," *Colorlines*, February 18, 2016, https://www.colorlines.com/articles/tbt-when-toni-morrison-checked-charlie-rose-white-privilege.

37   Rao, "Toni Morrison."

38   *Oxford English Dictionary*, s.v. "tokenism (*n.*)," accessed June 3, 2019, https://en.oxforddictionaries.com/definition/us/tokenism.

39   Eli Watkins and Abby Phillip, "Trump Decries Immigrants from 'Shithole Countries' Coming to US," CNN, January 12, 2018, https://www.cnn.com/2018/01/11/politics/immigrants-shithole-countries-trump/index.html.

40   Teju Cole, "The White-Savior Industrial Complex," *The Atlantic*, March 21, 2012, https://www.theatlantic.com/international/archive/2012/03/the-white-savior-industrial-complex/254843/.

41   Cole, "White-Savior Industrial Complex."

42   Constance Wu (@ConstanceWu), "Can We All at Least Agree," Twitter, July 29, 2016, 1:03 p.m., https://twitter.com/ConstanceWu/status/759086955816554496.

43   Robin DiAngelo, "White Fragility," *International Journal of Critical Pedagogy* 3, no. 3 (2011): 54–70.

44   Asam Ahmad, "A Note on Call-Out Culture," *Briarpatch*, March 2, 2015, https://briarpatchmagazine.com/articles/view/a-note-on-call-out-culture.

45   As quoted and paraphrased by Oprah, "Oprah Talks to Maya Angelou," *O Magazine*, May 2013, http://www.oprah.com/omagazine/maya-angelou-interviewed-by-oprah-in-2013.

46   Wikipedia, s.v. "Feminism," last modified June 2, 2019, 17:54, https://en.wikipedia.org/wiki/Feminism.

47   Wikipedia, s.v. "White Feminism," last modified June 3, 2019, 22:55, https://en.wikipedia.org/wiki/White_feminism.

48   bell hooks, *We Real Cool: Black Men and Masculinity* (New York: Routledge, 2004), 57.

49   Sally Roesch Wagner, ed., *The Women's Suffrage Movement* (New York: Penguin, 2019), 404.

50   J. D. Zahniser and Amelia R. Fry, *Alice Paul: Claiming Power* (Oxford: Oxford University Press, 2014), 138.

51   Emma Watson, "First Book of 2018! *Why I'm No Longer Talking to White People about Race* by Reni Eddo-Lodge," Our Shared Shelf announcements, Goodreads, December 31, 2017, https://www.goodreads.com/topic/show/19152741-first-book-of-2018-why-i-m-no-longer-talking-to-white-people-about-race.

52   Barbara C. Burrell, *Women and Political Participation: A Reference Handbook* (Santa Barbara, CA: ABC-CLIO, 2004), 185.

53   Sheila Thomas, "Intersectionality: The Double Bind of Race and Gender," *Perspectives* 2 (Spring 2004), https://www.americanbar.org/content/dam/aba/publishing/perspectives_magazine/women_perspectives_Spring2004CrenshawPSP.authcheckdam.pdf.

54   Emily Fornof, Nile Pierre, and Canela Lopez, "Kimberlé Crenshaw: Race Scholar Speaks on Erasure of Women of Color," *Tulane Hullabaloo*, October 4, 2017, https://tulanehullabaloo.com/30450/intersections/kimberle-crenshaw-3/.

55   The Circle Way website, http://www.thecircleway.net/.

56   Christina Baldwin and Ann Linnea, *The Circle Way: A Leader in Every Chair* (San Francisco: Berrett-Koehler Publishers, 2010), 144.

57   Alice Walker, *In Search of Our Mothers' Gardens* (Orlando, FL: Harcourt Inc., 1983), 290.

58   *Oxford English Dictionary*, s.v. "tokenism (*n.*)."

59   DiAngelo, *White Fragility*.

60   McIntosh, "White Privilege and Male Privilege."

acknowledgments

No creative work is accomplished in a vacuum, and no creator ever truly creates alone. It is my intention and desire that *Me and White Supremacy* is one part of my legacy that I leave behind as a living ancestor now and a good ancestor when I am gone. But I could not have done this work without the support and prayers of so many people, both in my personal community and in the global community.

Thank you, God, for the insight, patience, and love granted to do this work with integrity. Thank you to my husband, Sam, who since day one has been my biggest cheerleader, and to my children, Maya and Mohamed, who are my biggest inspirations. Thank you to my parents who instilled in me the importance of doing what it takes to leave this world better than I found it.

Thank you to my sacred circle of support, Sharona Lautoe, Leesa Renee Hall, Rasha Karim, Latham Thomas, Omkari Williams, and my mentor and friend Frantonia Pollins. Thank you to the Black educators, activists, and writers I have had the distinct honor of learning from and alongside in this challenging and important work.

Thank you to the literary ancestors who have influenced my healing as a Black woman and as a Black woman writer: Audre Lorde, Octavia Butler, and my daughter's namesake, Maya Angelou.

Thank you to my agent, Katherine Latshaw, and my editors at Sourcebooks, who have been instrumental in helping me transform *Me and White Supremacy*, the free digital workbook, into *Me and White Supremacy*, the expanded, published book. Words cannot express how grateful I am for the ways in which they have supported me and this work in becoming what it now is.

Thank you to the founders of The Circle Way process, Christina Baldwin and Ann Linnea, who have served as good ancestors to us all by laying out a process and a methodology for coming together in circle to do work that matters.

Lastly, thank you to everyone who has brought *Me and White Supremacy* into your personal lives, families, educational institutes, businesses, social spaces, worship spaces, nonprofits, communities, and industries. Thank you for not just reading the work but doing the work with the intention of creating a new world where Black, Indigenous, and People of Color live with dignity and equality.

about the author

LAYLA F. SAAD is a writer, speaker, and podcast host on the topics of race, identity, leadership, personal transformation, and social change.

As an East African, Arab, British, Black, Muslim woman who was born in and grew up in the UK and currently lives in Qatar, Layla has always sat at a unique intersection of identities from which she is able to draw rich and intriguing perspectives. Layla's work is driven by her powerful desire to "become a good ancestor," to live and work in ways that leave a legacy of healing and liberation for those who will come after she is gone.

Layla's work has been brought into communities, workplaces, institutions, and events around the world that are seeking to create personal and collective change.

Find out more about Layla at laylafsaad.com